BREAK

JENN DRUMMOND

PROOF

7 Strategies to Build Resilience
and Achieve Your Life Goals

BREAKPROOF

7 Strategies to Build Resilience and Achieve Your Life Goals

By Jenn Drummond

Coral Gables

For permission requests, please contact the publisher at:
Mango Publishing Group
2850 S Douglas Road, 2nd Floor
Coral Gables, FL 33134 USA
info@mango.bz

For special orders, quantity sales, course adoptions and corporate sales, please email the publisher at sales@mango.bz. For trade and wholesale sales, please contact Ingram Publisher Services at customer.service@ingramcontent.com or +1.800.509.4887.

BREAKPROOF: 7 STRATEGIES TO BUILD RESILIENCE AND ACHIEVE YOUR LIFE GOALS
Library of Congress Cataloging-in-Publication number: 2023941620
ISBN: 978-1-68481-435-0 (hardcover); 978-1-68481-436-7 (paperback); 978-1-68481-437-4 (e-book)
BISACs: SELF-HELP / Personal Growth / Success; SELF-HELP / Motivational & Inspirational; BUSINESS & ECONOMICS / Motivational

CONTENTS

CHAPTER 5: NAVIGATE THE MESSY MIDDLE

CHAPTER 6: RECOGNIZE WHEN IT ISN'T YOUR MOUNTAIN

CHAPTER 7: UNDERSTAND THAT THE GOAL IS NOT THE GOAL

CONCLUSION

Breakproof, *adj.*

refers to a resilient and adaptive mindset
that does not easily "break" under pressure,
reinterpreting the notion of quitting.

This perspective recognizes that our initial paths or methods might not always be the most fruitful or aligned with our long-term goals. As such, the capacity to reassess, recalibrate and, if necessary, redirect one's efforts is seen as a valuable asset. Instead of obstinately adhering to a task, goal, or plan—like sticking to a career path that is no longer fulfilling, even when it may no longer serve one's best interests—a breakproof approach values the ability to recognize when circumstances or objectives have changed. For instance, an individual with a breakproof mindset might reassess their professional trajectory when they notice a decline in their passion for their work, opting to pivot into a role or field that better aligns with their current interests and life circumstances.

Being breakproof isn't about mere persistence or blind allegiance to a course of action. Instead, it involves recognizing when to change strategies, similar to how a skilled sailor adjusts the sails to navigate changing winds effectively. This entails a continuous loop of self-evaluation—a process that might include regularly reviewing one's goals, assessing the alignment between current actions and those goals, seeking feedback from trusted colleagues or mentors, and reflecting on personal satisfaction and well-being. This iterative process ensures that one's actions and choices are dynamically responsive to evolving aspirations, strengths, and realities.

Life, with its vast array of experiences, lessons, and potential paths, demands a flexible navigation strategy. Challenges and setbacks aren't just hindrances—they are opportunities to accumulate wisdom, adapt, and potentially venture in a new direction; they allow for reinvention and growth. To be breakproof is to maintain a constant openness to new possibilities, such as taking a class in an unfamiliar subject, volunteering for a project outside of your usual scope at work, or networking with professionals in a different industry. This openness involves actively seeking opportunities for growth and being willing to step outside of one's comfort zone. This means ensuring that every step taken, whether it be advancing in a current career (a forward move), transitioning to a new field (a lateral move), or even taking a step back to learn and reassess (a backward move), is a purposeful decision aimed at fostering growth in both professional and personal dimensions such as acquiring new skills, improving mental well-being, or deepening relationships.

INTRODUCTION

LAX was no place to have a breakdown. Bustling crowds, constant motion, and an atmosphere of anxiety exuding from practically everyone racing to their gates—not exactly a safe place to find some refuge and reflect on one of the biggest disasters of my life. But after a chaotic flight back to the United States from Pakistan, all on the heels of a police escort and the very real loss of life, it was as close to a haven as I was going to get at that moment. I was desperate for sanctuary.

"I failed to summit; I just can't face my kids right now," I admitted over the phone to Karen, a thirty-three-year friend and our family's caregiver and house manager for over a decade. She had been acting as the emergency contact for my seven children while I was away on K2, and they were spending a month of their summer at three separate camps. Karen was understanding and sympathetic but couldn't comprehend what I had just been through. The truth was, I could hardly comprehend it. I needed time to process, come to terms with everything, and catch my breath. If possible, I needed time to make meaning out of it. I just needed time.

"Of course," Karen said, the consistent voice of reason and stability of our otherwise chaotic existence, no doubt hearing the emotion in my voice. "I've got everything covered here. The kids won't be home from camp for another few days anyway." Karen's response was a welcomed balm for my frayed nerves. At least everything was stable at home while I could decompress for a day or two.

I thought I had prepared for every challenge the journey would bring. Yet, I'd failed.

When I set out to climb the Seven Second Summits, I knew it wouldn't be like your average mom of seven setting a goal for herself. This was a life-and-death kind of challenge—one most wouldn't even consider. Expectations included minimal handholding, very few full nights of sleep, and the forgoing of all the creature comforts we typically associate with a comfortable life. Not to mention, eating very few square meals would be a necessary part of the plan. I wasn't naïve. I understood the physical toll—sores, aches, and the pervasive sand and snow. I was no stranger to discomfort and pain. I'd trained for this.

While climbing a mountain had its unique challenges, the ascent mirrored my experience in the corporate world: the highs and lows, the moments of doubt, and the elation of success. Both on the mountain and in business, conditions were unpredictable, tested my resilience, and pushed me to adapt. The altitude might be different, but the tenacity required was the same. This unyielding determination has been the cornerstone of my success, both in reaching the summits and building a business. For more than twenty years, I've carved my path as an entrepreneur. I founded a thriving financial-services firm through tenacity, perseverance, and an insane work ethic. I pursued these accomplishments to provide a comfortable lifestyle, afford my family's needs, and secure the financial resources necessary for an unprecedented adventure: to climb the second-highest peak on each of the seven continents—an incredible feat no woman had previously achieved.

By the time I'd made it to Pakistan, I'd already summited Mt. Everest (incidentally, not one of the Second Summits, but rather a challenge set forth by my youngest son on a bit of a dare nearly a year earlier) and come back in one piece. I thought I was well acquainted with discomfort and pain, well equipped with the necessary skills to take on another daring peak. Little did I know what lay ahead. K2 had its own set of unparalleled challenges.

Nothing had prepared me for Pakistan. I wasn't steeled against watching fellow climbers lose fingers to frostbite, enduring avalanches as frequent as wind gusts, or navigating the moral dilemma of mistrusting some of my porters—the very individuals tasked with guiding me safely to the summit. I especially never thought I'd be in a situation where I'd be burying a trusted friend who'd come to my aid in a previous climb but whose life was taken in an avalanche.

Still, all of the hardship was supposed to be worthwhile. All the sacrifices, the backbreaking climbs, and the deceptively treacherous trails were supposed to culminate in the clear, exhilarating view from a mountain's peak, though we don't climb for the view. We climb to prove we are alive and capable of overcoming. The will of the human spirit has no adversary.

But I didn't summit.

I'd failed. I'd lost. I'd quit. I felt on the brink of breaking.

I knew I was being a little hard on myself. Success is not the same as summiting. After all, who we are as people is more important than what we achieve. And I wasn't the kind who just gave up, especially after all the work and sacrifice to get to that point. This expedition had thrown more than enough grief our way, and the team elected to turn around—for all the right reasons.

But despite the decision having been a collective one, I still battled with that malicious little voice in the back of my head saying, "You quit. And as a result, you didn't summit the second-highest peak in Asia." The weight of the situation was overwhelming.

Of course, K2 was more than just a mountain to me. It symbolized a mother wrestling with her dreams, a public figure facing her critics, and a human standing up to intense fear. It was also a test of the principles that had brought me success as a self-made entrepreneur. My mountain-climbing quest was all of that and more, and I had quit. No wonder it hit me so hard.

But then I had a real-time epiphany. Maybe I didn't quit. Maybe I merely stopped; paused.

In a state of indescribable fear, pain, anxiety, and mental anguish on K2, I reconnected to my governing value: "People over peaks." No mountain—literal or metaphorical—is more important than people. All people. The porters, sherpas, base-camp managers, climbing partners, and guides. We'd chosen what was best for the team.

I didn't quit. I didn't break. I stopped.

Quitting means no longer expanding and growing, and I had done—and would continue to do—plenty of that. I had stopped, and now I needed to recalibrate strategically to move forward and find new perspectives. Because sometimes you need to climb down in order to climb back up.

In the ensuing year, I grappled with my failure. Even as I managed to tick two more climbs off my list in my quest to become the world-record holder as the first woman in history to climb the Seven Second Summits, K2 gnawed at the back of my brain. Why had everything gone so wrong? Could I fathom going back after what happened the year before? Was turning around a mistake? Was I even cut out for this? Was it worth the struggle, training, and grueling toll on my mind, body, and soul? What was I supposed to learn from all of this?

Quitting means no longer expanding and growing.

Was it even possible for someone to become breakproof? Mentally? Emotionally? Physically? Spiritually? Professionally? What would it mean to become breakproof?

Through my experiences on and off the mountains, I've come to understand a great deal about quitting (or "breaking") and the resilience we can build to become breakproof. Whether you're a business leader facing your own summits or frustrations with your team, a parent struggling to balance all the requirements of raising kids in today's world, or if you're just tired of existing on the couch and you want to embrace a bigger, even life-changing physical goal, I've written this book for you. While my journey may seem unique, the lessons I've derived have a universal appeal. Whether you're climbing a literal mountain or facing a personal or professional uphill battle, the heart of the journey—the core challenges and rewards—remains the same.

Mountaineering is undoubtedly part of the laboratory of my experience and an apt metaphor to lean into throughout this book. Still, the principles and practices are equally grounded in my experiences building a multimillion-dollar business and raising seven humans to be responsible and contributing citizens. You likely have a symbolic mountain to climb of your own, or perhaps you're responsible for others as a leader or parent. If my real-world adventures—sometimes harrowing and sometimes inspiring—serve as a catalyst and encourage you to venture into the wilderness of your fears and doubts, I'll count that as a good thing.

If you read and apply the lessons I've learned, I hope you might find ways to confront failures, learn from them, and develop resilience in your journey.

Because a year later, I did summit K2.

How I got there—including the seven strategies I learned to ultimately overcome that failure—is your invitation to read on, to overcome the complex challenges that stand between you and what matters most to you, to become breakproof.

CHAPTER 1

CAST YOUR VISION
WIDER AND DEEPER

MT. TYREE

Landing a plane in Antarctica is like landing on a mirror, where the glistening, reflective surface blurs the discernment of depth or solidity. The landscape is one constant sheet—illusory, constantly challenging the boundaries between the earth and sky, leaving pilots navigating a fine line between tangible reality and deceptive reflection. There's no runway, no control tower, and no lights guiding your descent down the most inhospitable landmass on the planet; you get none of the luxuries every other airport affords. Without the typical markers and comforts of a standard airport, landing calls for acute precision, expert judgment, and the ability to make split-second decisions amid uncertainty—attributes pilots must possess and that we, too, often need to navigate life's unpredictable terrains.

The journey to Antarctica begins in Chile, the sole gateway to the southernmost point of our planet, where flights operate not on a fixed schedule but at the mercy of the weather's whim. This level of unpredictability adds a unique twist to what is already a challenging endeavor. Planes only take off when the sun is projected to be in a perfect position—one that will allow your plane to cast a delineating shadow on the white stretch of ice. That's all the help you get to land an aircraft in Antarctica: a fleeting shadow in the blinding whiteness. And if you take off from Punta Arenas and a random cloud comes into view, or headwinds are strong enough that you miss your window, you have to turn around and head straight back. That means you have to fly a large, fuel-efficient aircraft, prepared for the possibility of returning to Chile without ever touching ground in Antarctica. It's an exercise in navigating through uncertainty, much like charting a path toward a goal in life without a clear map or guide. It's challenging, demands precision, and sometimes feels nearly impossible. It's a daring gamble against nature that requires nerves of steel and unwavering trust in one's skills and equipment.

I'm getting a little ahead of myself. Before I delved into the arduous journey of landing a plane in Antarctica, I should have introduced you to the reason for this journey: my Antarctic adversary, Mt. Tyree. At a height of 4,852 meters (15,919 feet), Mt. Tyree sits just a hair below the highest peak in Antarctica, Mt. Vinson at 4,892 meters (16,050 feet). To prepare for Mt. Tyree, we summited Mt. Vinson first and made our way to Mt. Tyree a week later. While these two peaks are only 130 feet apart, making them almost indistinguishable in height, they differ significantly in difficulty—not just because of less climbing but because of Mt. Tyree's mostly unexplored terrain.

That's the kind of backward thing about Second Summits. Most people hear "the Seven Second Summits" and wonder why anyone would stop at the *second*-highest peak in each continent. "What? Couldn't you hack the highest summit? Must not have been good enough to climb the tallest mountains." Listen, climbing a mountain is hard. Climbing *any* mountain is hard. What makes any climb easier is when someone has gone before you.

Climbing the Seven Summits (the tallest mountain on each of the seven continents) is no easy feat, and it's many mountaineers' dream. Who hasn't wanted to climb Mt. Everest or Mt. Kilimanjaro? In total (depending on whom you ask), about five hundred people have climbed all Seven Summits, and the number grows every year. Because of the commercial appeal of these mountains, tourism, branding, and climbing guides have sprung up left and right around these pursuits.

The base camps are what some might call "glamping": fresh meals and more pack animals than a petting zoo. Depending on their topography, some of the Seven Summits are more difficult than others. For example, Mt. Everest would be an almost impossible feat if it weren't for the commercialization. However, since it's been commercialized, it has become a much more straightforward and attainable feat.

In many ways, climbing the Seven *Second* Summits is much harder than the Seven Summits, given the added challenges of fewer amenities and resources and the lesser-trodden paths that come with pursuing these less-commercialized peaks. The commercial difference between the highest and second-highest peaks could be compared to the money spent on the major leagues and junior leagues of sports teams in the United States. Because commercialization is much lower for these mountains, there's far less help provided. To put things into perspective, Mt. Vinson, the tallest mountain in Antarctica, is attempted by approximately 150–200 people per season. Mt. Tyree gets one team of 5 people per season, and that's it. Aside from me, only one person on record has completed the Seven Second Summits.

The appeal of the highest peaks casts a shadow over their lesser counterparts, but this does not diminish their challenge or the allure they hold for some climbers. I was drawn to a path that far fewer have traveled. In these lesser-known, formidable climbs, I found my vision stretching wider, encompassing a broader view of the world's grand peaks, and deeper into the soul of why we climb. The Seven Second Summits whispered to my spirit of exploration—they aren't just the "second best"; their mystery is part of their allure, their untouched majesty beckoning and daunting.

Looking Out for the Next Climbers

Mt. Vinson has multiple teams attempting to summit it each season. It has an established base camp staffed with a chef and extra guides in the event of an emergency. The first group to ascend will set the path for that year and secure ropes in the dangerous sections for others to follow. Every few days, new teams come to climb, teams that have completed their quest are picked up, and base camp is replenished with supplies. Despite the established routine and support at Mt. Vinson, climbing this mountain was still a substantial undertaking. On my climb, I got more than my fair share of blisters, enough to have new boots flown in before attempting Mt. Tyree a week later.

Mt. Tyree was a different beast altogether. Its challenge lay not only in its physical demands but also in the mental and logistical challenges of attempting a peak that few have set their sights on. Mt. Tyree was another thirty-minute plane ride away from Mt. Vinson, and our drop-off spot was where the plane stopped after landing. We unloaded gear, stomped down snow to make a level surface to set up tents, and watched that little tin can of a plane fly off. The remoteness sunk in. No chef. No established camps. No tracks to follow. No animals. No plants. No colors. Nothing and nobody but us in the stark, pure wilderness. And if there were an emergency, we'd have to wait over an hour for a plane to get to us, and that plane could only fly if the weather were perfect.

This place was the epitome of uncharted territory. Aside from the four guides with me (that's right, four guides for one climber) and the twenty or so people who had gone before us, we were blazing our own route. Well, we weren't so much blazing a trail as we were carefully etching our path into the icy slopes.

Lucky for us, one of the guides on my team had been one of the previous summiters, so in addition to his memory, we relied on all the notes, photos, and scribbles people left to guide us. But here's the catch: The mountain was still a mystery in many ways, having not been summited since 2019. We faced the unknown: How had the conditions changed over the years? Would there be more snow or ice this year? Would the rock they used to secure a rope be buried, or could we access it? Likewise, taking advice from those who have achieved the same goals you're reaching for under different conditions and circumstances can come with a grain of salt. Just because they succeeded in a particular way doesn't mean you will. In everything from personal growth to business ventures, the environment can change enough that you can't follow someone's guidance too strictly. At times like those, relying solely on others might prove detrimental. Instead, it's essential to adapt and use your best judgment.

But any advice is better than no advice. We took it graciously and planned to pass it on. Combining more notes from more expeditions solidifies the accuracy for the next group. After all, ten people's notes and experiences are more valuable than two. And by notes, of course I mean records of details like the thickness of a rope, the distance between ice screws, and drawings and pictures (if there were still life in our phones). Similarly, as you navigate your path toward your goals, remember to leave "notes" for those who follow you. Sharing your experiences, triumphs, and failures not only helps others but can also give you a new perspective on your journey.

Focused by Default

Our climb of Mt. Tyree was marked by three significant milestones: base camp, Camp 1, and the ultimate goal: the summit. With the base camp established, it was time to focus on the next camp, Camp 1. We knew its proximity and devised a strategy to get there. Our guide's experience was invaluable. It allowed us to focus our energy on our direction rather than second-guessing every move. This efficiency saved time and energy, key commodities when striving to become breakproof.

As you might guess, Antarctica is a vast expanse of uninhabitable barren ice and packed snow. There's no natural vegetation or wildlife. Sounds come from you or the wind, and colors are limited to that of the blue sky, yellow sun, black rock, and white snow. The simplicity of this setting can be both a boon and a curse. Without a doubt, the mountains in Antarctica come with the fewest distractions. Even in camp, there are few chores, except managing your gear and melting water. The almost complete absence of distractions allowed all our efforts to be channeled toward this one goal. Becoming breakproof—developing the resilience and determination to see a challenge through to the end—is easier when fewer distractions pull our focus away. When you can focus wholeheartedly on the task at hand, you spend all your energy problem-solving and strategizing, which is beneficial both on mountains and in our everyday pursuits in life. The challenge lies in maintaining that singular focus without getting overwhelmed. The sheer emptiness of the place—both expected and surprising—can weigh on one's psyche.

Mt. Tyree presents a formidable ascent, its slopes rise sharply with an average incline of around 60 percent, akin to scaling a near-vertical wall. It's a beast of a challenge. That means rather than your typical hike, you're climbing with ice axes as walking sticks (to help in the event you slip and need to self-arrest) and crampons (metal claws you attach to the bottom of your boots) that allow you to stick to the mountain. The tools are not just aids, they are lifelines. On the bright side, there's minimal chance for avalanches at that incline.

Most of the climb felt like a StairMaster, yet we roped off to one another for safety reasons. Every movement demanded the utmost precision. In such an unforgiving terrain, a single misstep would spell disaster. We broke into two smaller climbing teams to move quickly and efficiently. Each pitch was around 50–60 meters (55–65 yards) and was usually climbed by one person at a time. So we had plenty of time to catch our breath before we would have to go again. This approach wasn't just about conserving stamina; it was a calculated strategy for survival, carefully balancing our physical exertion with the need to remain alert and responsive in the harsh environment.

When stress is low, that's when it's best to prepare for difficulties that will eventually arise.

We appreciated how smoothly things were going, knowing that challenges could always present themselves. When stress is low, that's when it's best to prepare for difficulties that will eventually arise.

Arming yourself with the right tools and staying disciplined in all the steps helps minimize the magnitude of the trickier sections.

We made it to Camp 1, set up camp, and got ready for the next day. But resting wasn't just about physical recovery; it was mentally gearing up for what lay ahead. After a night spent tossing and turning due to the biting cold and our anxious anticipation, we began our prolonged climb to the summit, following a path similar to the previous day's but extending far longer. Because of the way Mt. Tyree stands, there's only one spot on the mountain where any camp can be set up, and it's not that far up the mountain. The climb from base camp to Camp 1 takes roughly six hours, which isn't long. Because of that, the summit day is much longer, taking about eighteen hours to go from Camp 1 to the summit and back down to Camp 1.

We started our ascent as usual. Crampon, crampon; ice ax, ice ax. Again and again. Crampon, crampon; ice ax, ice ax. We were methodically making our way up the mountain. That day we scaled twenty-two pitches, tapping on ice, weaving around rocks, and etching our progress into the ice like little tally marks. One tick mark at a time. We stuck to the plan and made adjustments as obstacles arose. You can almost always count on obstacles, but it's how you overcome them that becomes part of the game and the adventure.

Of course, significant obstacles also make their way into our lives, and the most significant obstacle I'd face on Mt. Tyree lay in the homestretch just before it was time to walk the ridgeline: blue ice.

Changing Pace

The crux of a climb refers to its most challenging part. On Mt. Tyree, this crux was a daunting stretch of dark-blue, virtually impenetrable ice. When it gets really cold, like Antarctic cold, and water freezes solidly, the unyielding ice takes on a dark-blue hue. Imagine facing a path of unbreakable ice while charting your course to the summit of a mountain. Unlike more porous ice or snow-covered terrains that provide some traction or potential footholds, this dense ice offers none. This is the moment where the pace changes, where every decision becomes a negotiation with the ice. Every movement must be calculated and deliberate, each step or grip echoing with sharp clicks and crunches against the solidified barrier. I knew I had to think creatively, employing more precision and climbing on all fours.

A sinking feeling settled in my stomach. "Great, I've physically become an animal to make progress."

When climbing blue ice, the level of mental precision required is akin to that of a brain surgeon—any less, and the ice will ruthlessly reject your efforts. You will slide till the rope you are tied to stops your fall. This late in the climb means it's time to refocus, slow down, and rely on technical grace. It reminded me of how, when you get into a dicey situation you may not have foreseen, slowing down and ensuring you're being precise is your best strategy forward. Just as in climbing, life's path has its own "blue ice" sections—those daunting, unexpected challenges that demand our full attention and skill. The question that looms is: Are you prepared for when these challenges show up?

When climbing a mountain, I have to remind myself that the summit wasn't home, and home was the ultimate goal. This distinction helps keep climbers grounded in their motivations. I had to check in with myself at several points along the way. Do I have enough energy to make it home from here? Can we continue forward and still make it to base camp safely? Just as I needed to constantly assess my limits to ensure I could make the descent safely after reaching the summit, I imagine a similar principle applies in the business world: continuously evaluating resources and strategies to reach a high point and sustain it. I often wonder how many businesses would still be around if they checked in to make sure they could "make it home" from where they were on their mountain.

We were tantalizingly close to the summit. Yet, with the most challenging part of the climb still ahead, I could feel a new raw edge to my determination. Focus, precision, and intentionality were key to making progress. This phase required every ounce of mental fortitude.

I chose to go last in this section, allowing me to study the marks made by those before me. Their paths served as a guide, offering insights into the ice's quirks and helping me choose my placements more accurately—a tangible benefit of following in experienced footsteps.

Once the blue ice was behind us, a wave of relief washed over me. The path ahead, though still demanding, now seemed less menacing. With summit fever kicking in, the mountain seemed to pull us upward, inviting us closer to its peak. After a grueling struggle against time, the elements, and my own limits, finally—and on New Year's Day, of all days—I stood at the summit.

The View From the Top

You celebrate reaching the summit of a mountain because it represents the culmination of everything that has come before—your journey, struggles, and triumphs; all the challenges you overcame; all the mental gymnastics you played to continue, even as every atom in your body was screaming for you to turn around. It proves that you can do hard things. It shows that you are capable of more than you ever imagined. At the top of the mountain, for a single breath in and out, time disappears, and you are the energetic force of life, one with all. With each exhale, you feel grounded; yet, you also sense a part of your spirit soaring, reconnecting you with the world in its most vibrant form. You did it. You made it to the top. All that hard work, pain, stress, and planning worked out.

The summit reminds you that when you are fueled with purpose, you never truly run out of energy. It's a testament to human perseverance and determination. Because each breath in gives you the ability to go one step further. And all pursuits are climbed one step at a time.

As you descend, you carry a new wisdom: You are built to conquer mountains. With one peak behind you, it's time to use what you've learned as you embark on your next adventure.

BE BREAKPROOF: HOW TO CAST YOUR VISION WIDER AND DEEPER

1. **Establish Clear Goals and Milestones.** Define your larger vision and break it down into smaller, manageable steps or landmarks. This makes progress more visible and achievable. Connect with your motivations and passions when establishing your goals and milestones. Use these as fuel to propel you forward. Tap into the energetic force of life and utilize it to experience the world in its fullest expression. This could mean channeling your passions, using your emotions as a driving force, or simply harnessing your innate energy to power through challenges. Define your larger vision with ambition and realism, breaking it down into smaller, achievable steps or landmarks.

2. **Learn From Others' Experiences.** Utilize the knowledge and experiences of those who have gone before you as a guide. Their "notes" can provide valuable insights, even if they don't apply directly to your current circumstances. The knowledge and skills of those more experienced in your field or pursuit can help you anticipate challenges, improve your strategies, avoid common pitfalls, and propel you in the right direction. The more perspectives and experiences you can gather, the more accurate your decisions will likely be. This enhances your vision, making it wider and deeper. Seeking out diverse voices will ensure a more comprehensive understanding. Always critically evaluate others' experiences, as their lessons may not directly apply to your unique situation.

3. **Share Your Own Experiences.** Your own experiences, successes, and failures can provide valuable lessons for others. Sharing these can also help you reflect on your journey and gain new perspectives. Use the knowledge and wisdom you've gained from your journey to prepare for future adventures. Every experience provides valuable lessons that can be applied to future pursuits. When sharing your experiences, ensure that you communicate your lessons with clarity and relevance, offering actionable insights for others.

4. **Be Adaptable to Change.** Recognize that conditions and circumstances can change, making it impossible to strictly follow someone else's guidance. It's crucial to adapt and use your best judgment based on the current situation. You may encounter unexpected obstacles on your journey. In such moments, creativity and resourcefulness will be your greatest assets. Adapt to changing circumstances and maintain a well-thought-out plan as your guiding structure. Adaptability shouldn't be an excuse for lack of planning.

5. **Minimize Distractions.** Foster an environment allowing focused effort toward your goal. Be specific about what these distractions are and implement practical measures to mitigate them. Reducing distractions will enable you to concentrate all your energy on the task at hand.

6. **Apply Consistent Effort and Discipline.** Uphold a level of discipline in your steps and remain consistent in your actions. Consistent, small efforts over time can lead to significant results. Discipline involves precision and care. Particularly in tricky situations, precision and careful decision making are crucial. Sometimes, slowing down and focusing on the details can lead to the best way forward.

7. **Understand Your Environment.** Comprehend the complexities and nuances of the environment you're working within. Do thorough research and always be open to learning. Whether it's physical or metaphorical, understanding your terrain can help you navigate it more effectively. Seek expert advice when unsure.

8. **Prioritize Safety and Sustainability.** Always monitor your ability to sustain your effort and return "home." Develop a contingency plan for potential risks. This includes ensuring your physical well-being and maintaining the resources needed to continue your pursuit in the long term.

9. **Acknowledge Your Strength and Celebrate Your Achievements.** Realize that achieving your goals can be a testament to your power and potential. This understanding can sometimes be more intimidating than failure, but it's important

to embrace it. Recognize and celebrate the challenges you have overcome. This boosts your confidence and reinforces your belief in your ability to accomplish demanding tasks.

10. **Embrace the Moment.** Live in the present and fully appreciate each success, no matter how small, as you work toward your larger goal. It's a chance to connect with your deepest self and the world around you. However, while introspection is essential, it shouldn't deter you from the next steps. Seek a balance between reflection and action to continue your forward momentum.

YOUR VISION FOR YOUR MOUNTAIN

You might think my experience climbing Mt. Tyree has little relevance to your life. Well, Mt. Tyree is a symbol for the process of goal setting. The parallel here is that just like the physical act of climbing requires vision and careful planning, setting—and achieving—your goals requires the same foresight and attention to detail. The key is to understand that we are born with the ability to envision our future—to dream, set goals, and see connections that might not be immediately obvious. We are creators, and those brave enough to bring

When you set big goals, there might not always be a clear path or set of instructions to follow. But that doesn't mean you're lost.

our visions to life become breakproof. We set a goal, achieve it, and come home to reach for new mountains, applying the lessons we've learned to our future endeavors. We apply our experiences in our lives, marking milestones and sharing our wisdom to help others expand their horizons.

While this book primarily addresses the adventure of climbing physical mountains, its deeper meaning is metaphorical. We are all on individual journeys, facing ascents and descents as we strive toward our personal and professional peaks. Drawing from the extremes of the Antarctic, my lessons can equip you for your journey. Just as I faced a literal barren tundra, you, too, will face unforgiving landscapes on the path to achieving your goals. This book is for those setting ambitious goals, whether personal, professional, or both. It is for anyone trying to grasp a vision for a brighter future, hoping to leave a legacy behind, and struggling to make their dreams a reality. And that all starts with learning how to expand your vision.

Just as navigating the ever-changing terrain of Mt. Tyree was a challenge, life, too, can feel like an unmarked route. When you set big goals, there might not always be a clear path or set of instructions to follow. But that doesn't mean you're lost. And more often than not, there will be something you don't expect, and being staunch in adhering to your original vision can cause you to miss your ultimate destination. Because becoming breakproof doesn't mean you're insolent or stubborn; rather, it implies a steadfast dedication to overcoming challenges in pursuit of something meaningful. It indicates you've committed to something worthy of accomplishing that challenges you to learn and grow.

And perhaps that's where the joy of life comes in: learning to dance through the storms of life and turning those perceived setbacks into stepping stones toward your goals. Ultimately, you become adaptable and resilient, not by avoiding discomfort but by learning to use that discomfort as fuel to ignite your creativity and drive.

For the rest of this chapter, I will unpack what I learned from this experience and show how those lessons can help you achieve your goals. Keep in mind, no matter what you want to achieve, learning from those who have walked the same road (or any difficult path) will help you get started on the right foot. So let's start walking.

Who Said It Best?

My goal was to become the first woman to climb to the top of the Seven Second Summits. However, not every goal I've made has been a "first to do" kind of goal, and I'm guessing neither are many of yours. Standing at the forefront isn't always the driving force behind our ambitions. Whether starting a business, inventing a product, writing a book, or learning a new challenging skill, other entrepreneurs, inventors, authors, and creators have gone before you, and their wisdom is to your benefit. In ways large and small, their work will have become the foundation necessary to take your ideas where they need to go.

The Seven Second Summits was my medium to illustrate what happens when you shed limiting beliefs and become breakproof, developing a relentless, unwavering determination in your pursuits. It's about sharing the lessons I have learned so that when something tugs at your heart, you have the courage, patience, and perseverance to bring it to life. Your path will inevitably look different from those who have gone before, but the knowledge gained from those before will still guide you forward.

Here's the thing, though: Even if your goal isn't about being the "first" in the world to accomplish something, it will always be a "first" for you—and that in itself is immensely valuable. There's still plenty to be gained from experts in your field. For instance, I wasn't the first woman to summit each mountain I climbed. (The closest I came to that was Mt. Tyree, where I was the second woman to summit successfully.) I was, however, the first American woman and the first amateur woman to summit Mt. Tyree. (The previous woman is a licensed guide.) I am incredibly grateful to her and the other climbers who summited Tyree before me. Without their insight, the route up would have been much more difficult; the insights I gained from their experiences were individual stepping stones, guiding me to approach my goal one step at a time. So my advice is this: Become a student of life so that when faced with challenges, you will take that knowledge and continue on. No matter your goal, progress forward.

Look at the people who have gone before you—research pioneers and experts who have achieved your goal or have excelled in a related field. You can look up interviews or biographies. They may have even blogged or vlogged their journey, which would be very insightful. If you're lucky, you might even get them to mentor you. The woman who climbed Mt. Tyree before me brought her laptop and showed me pictures of different parts of the mountain I was to watch out for. I got to ask her about gear, food, weather, temperature, and more. Her insight and expertise helped ease my nerves as to what to expect. Seeing environments through an expert's eyes allows us to frame them in our minds. Even if the route ahead is like Mt. Tyree, with few natural landmarks, you'll recognize different points that otherwise would have seemed mundane and unremarkable. Having that foresight helps give us reference points to document progress in our pursuits.

As you delve into the lives and journeys of these trailblazers, consider the following questions to guide your exploration: How did they prepare to achieve this goal? How did they feel while they were in the middle of it? Whom did they rely on for guidance? Whom did they rely on for support? What did they talk about afterward? Did they have any regrets? epiphanies? What would they have done differently if given the chance to do it again? What inspired them to push through the tough times?

Whether your ambition is as specific as opening an authentic Parisian café or as broad as starting a financial services business, your journey will be uniquely yours. No matter your goal—you stand to gain immensely from seeking advice and wisdom from those who have tread similar paths, even if their journey wasn't identical to the one you envision.

It's worth noting that you may look back and realize what you've done before has perfectly prepared you for this next goal in your life. However, even if your past seems unrelated to your new dream, remember that every skill you've learned and every challenge you've faced has contributed to who you are today. You are always equipped to begin. For instance, I had no clue I wanted to get into mountain climbing, but when I looked at my past activities, they laid a solid foundation as a mountain climber. Get curious about the experiences you yearn for in life and the knowledge you hope to acquire. Trust that these pieces, although they might seem unrelated now, will come together meaningfully in your future.

If you're interested in blazing new routes in your own life, study those who have pioneered in other careers. Their strategies, resilience, and wisdom are your tools too. By seeking guidance from those who came before us, we become part of a lineage of dreamers and doers, and in doing so, we turn our unique visions into our individual realities.

Take It One Step at a Time

Consider this: Each step while you're climbing is actually four steps: crampon, crampon; ice ax, ice ax. Now imagine if every time you walked down the street, you had to strap down each of your feet, double-check that your hands were still at your side, and stay on the lookout for the sidewalk potentially collapsing from under you with every step. You'd never go anywhere! A walk around the block would take an hour!

Crampon, crampon; ice ax, ice ax. Despite the grind, I found ways to make ice climbing fun. **The main key was perspective.** A positive attitude and wild imagination are your best weapons against the drone of monotony. If you shift your focus from wondering *if* you'll achieve your goal and instead focus on how much fun you're having *while* achieving your goal, you'll progress toward your destination faster and with greater confidence. For example, when we had to flatten the snow at base camp to set up our tents, I was reminded of building snow forts as a kid in Michigan. Suddenly, this dry, flavorless task became a game, and I caught myself grinning as I stomped the snow flat. This was my dream as a five-year-old, and here I was as a forty-something living it to the fullest. How lucky I was! Changing how you view a task, from a burden to an opportunity for enjoyment or reflection, can transform the entire experience.

Despite the extreme cold in Antarctica, the physical exhaustion of the climb, and the intense moments of isolation from climbing one at a time, it was easy to have a positive attitude also because **I'd broken the climb down into manageable pieces.** I was constantly achieving little goals. On Mt. Tyree, zooming out my vision to view the entire 100-foot pitch might have helped me foresee a way up, but it wasn't what provided a sense of accomplishment throughout the process.

A positive attitude and wild imagination are your best weapons against the drone of monotony.

Zooming in to the next step—breaking 100 feet down to 8- to 12-inch increments—gave me a sense of accomplishment every minute or so. It made the vast and daunting climb feel like a series of small, manageable victories.

When you first set a goal for yourself, start by mapping out a path to achieving that goal. Seeing a way to the top is pivotal to achieving success because it provides a clear direction and motivation, anchoring you during tough times and fueling your determination. And once you have that initial path laid out, break down that path into smaller goals and steps. If your goal is to launch a new product line in your business, start by conducting a market analysis. Next, determine the resources needed, create a prototype or a pilot version, and gather feedback. Then, establish a timeline for production, marketing, and distribution. Some of the best entrepreneurs break down their business plans into even more manageable chunks. "First, finalize the product design based on feedback. Now, collaborate with the marketing team to devise a launch strategy. Done? Now, organize events or webinars to introduce the product to potential clients." And so on. This way, the business venture doesn't feel like a monolithic task but a series of small, achievable distances. Taking your goal one step at a time will make it easier to manage and be more enjoyable. Checking off a box on your to-do list is satisfying. It gives you a little burst of serotonin every time you do it; the chemicals throughout your body reward you for a job well done. When you achieve small goals, you give yourself more opportunities to reward and reinforce the behavior that gets you closer to your goal. And the more you reward yourself, the more likely you are to keep pushing onward and upward. So here's your challenge: Start envisioning your goal, break it down into achievable steps, and take that first bold stride toward your dreams. Remember, every monumental journey begins with a single, purposeful step—and don't forget to have fun along the way.

Plan for "Now What?"

Then comes the blue ice—dense, hard, and slick: one of the most treacherous terrains to navigate.

In life, "blue ice" represents those unexpected and challenging situations that catch you off guard. No matter how well you plan and how many little goals you set for yourself, there will inevitably come a hitch, a bump in the road, or a hurdle to leap over (pick your favorite metaphor). No climb is without surprises. No matter how easy the road looks ahead, something unexpected may come your way. Every goal you strive for will come with blue ice. And here's the good news: that's okay! While you can't always predict challenges, you can prepare for the "what if?" parts of the climb. And that is the difference in whether someone summits the mountain or not. It is crucial to adapt to challenges when they show up.

I was lucky to have expert guides along the way. They shared vital tips on how to look for the right indicators that I was succeeding: the color of the ice to strike at, the sound the ice ax would make when it stuck in just right, and which angle gave the best leverage. But even with guidance, I had to learn how to climb blue ice on the fly, which required immediate adaptation—no easy feat. What helped me through it was planning for something like this to happen. This was my fourth Second Summit, and I was no stranger at this point to changes in plans. Something often goes wrong, whether it's a change in weather, the usual route becoming unusable, or a climber getting sick or injured. I had to infuse my vision with flexibility. If I had been dead set on ice-climbing my way to Mt. Tyree's summit the way I knew how, I would never have made it to the top. But ice climbing wasn't the goal; Mt. Tyree was.

Problems come up. That's life! Achieving your goals isn't a matter of luck—it's a matter of confronting and navigating the realities of life. Do you have the right gear, circumstances, and environment to succeed? Recall a specific time when you were working toward a significant goal. What was your "blue ice" moment during that journey? What unexpected obstacle got in your way where you had to change tactics? These kinds of obstacles are the ones that can't be avoided but require ingenuity and adaptation to work through them. Like my blue-ice experience, they require deliberate changes in strategy and precision in your execution. In these times, progress may go slower than you're used to, but the summit is still getting closer. It's just a matter of adapting to the obstacles at hand.

Keep your plans flexible, like a climber who keeps their knees relaxed, ready to sidestep when a rock falls. This means being prepared to adjust your strategy when unexpected challenges arise. And when those obstacles get in your way, you'll be able to focus on what's truly important and approach your goal from a different angle. Because at the end of the day, it's not just about reaching the top—it's about the lessons learned and the person you become on your way there.

Look Back, Look Forward

Mt. Tyree is so remote and inaccessible that any detail for the route ahead is pure gold. Getting to the top of Mt. Tyree required looking back; this meant studying the routes and strategies of climbers before me. It also required that I look forward to those climbing it the following season. And the season after that, and the one after that. As great as it felt to receive precious advice from previous climbers, I realized the importance of paying this knowledge forward. Taking my own notes and recording the nuances of the route felt like creating magic, a guidebook for future adventurers. These invaluable resources meant I hadn't climbed this mountain just for myself. My legacy wouldn't only be a world record, it would be lights illuminating the way for others who would come after me.

It can be easy to get caught in the trap of self-centeredness when pursuing your own goals. After all, *you* are the one achieving this goal. *You* are the one facing the difficulties and coming out on top. While it may feel like you are the central figure in your quest, remember the timeless truth: No man is an island. Our successes are collective victories shaped and supported by those around us. Achieving any goal requires a team behind an individual. There's no way around it. We're social creatures, and we live in a society. Taking care of each other is part of the deal.

Think back to a big goal you achieved. Now, consider the people who were part of that journey—family, friends, mentors. When climbing any mountain, the number of people you think contributed starts small and expands exponentially the more you think about it. On this climb, I had four guides to help me. Then there were also the experts at ALE (Antarctic Logistics and Expeditions) that provided invaluable logistical and weather forecasting support. And I can't forget the pilots who flew me from Chile to Antarctica and those who further flew me to the base of Mt. Tyree. What about all the people who designed, manufactured, and sold me all of my gear? The companies that made the crampons, gloves, ropes, and my tent all had a hand in my success. That's the nature of goals. No one ever does it alone.

Regardless of its scale, every goal carries lessons and insights that can be invaluable for others on a similar path. As others contribute to your vision becoming a reality, it's essential to weave a commitment to giving back into that vision. If you'd like to participate in this cycle of learning and teaching actively, you might consider options like keeping a journal, starting a blog, or recording your training sessions. These aren't requirements but opportunities to enrich your journey and potentially inspire others. At the very least, be intentional in remembering the most important steps you took along the way. Your journey, when shared, becomes more than a personal achievement; it empowers others to embark on their remarkable quests. As you climb your mountains, I challenge you to document your journey. Share your struggles and triumphs, for in doing so, you light the path for others and continue a legacy of collective achievement. Ultimately, by sharing your journey, you enrich others' visions and, in turn, broaden your own.

You Can Only See So Much; You Can Only See So Far

In the biting cold of Antarctica, the stark white landscape muffled sounds, and the icy air left no scent. Climbing Mt. Tyree was more than a physical endeavor—every frosty breath reminded me of my determination; every muscle ache was a testament to my commitment. This climb required my full presence, my fears and hopes, my resolve and vulnerability. It asked me to be wholly there, body and soul. It taught me a profound lesson in focus; it demanded my attention to be in the present, on each step directly in front of me. I call this the "Be where your feet are" concept, which means to remain fully engaged and present in the current moment. It is the practice of grounding oneself, not letting the mind wander into the future or the past but focusing on the current task or situation. This is a lesson I took to heart. It's about being mindful of the step you are taking now rather than worrying about the entire journey ahead. While keeping long-term vision in perspective, you're not allowing it to become a distraction. Even though I had three more peaks on my list after Mt. Tyree, including a second attempt at K2, I knew that planning for those future climbs during my ascent would only distract me, taking my mind off the crucial decisions and actions required at that very moment.

Learn to focus on the details directly before you so you don't slip on your route to your goals.

The other side of that coin is the reminder that there will always be another goal to chase after the one right before you. Mt. Tyree was a formidable goal in and of itself, and if I only climbed this mountain and none other, it would still be a great story. However, giving myself the smallest reminder that there were other mountains to climb (while not dwelling on the logistics of those mountains) gave me hope for what would come after I summited. Without that, I may have become hopeless or anxious when approaching the end of my expedition.

Keeping secondary goals—objectives that are meaningful but separate from your primary aim—will help ease your anxiety in the present. Without these other goals, you may end up inside your head: what happens when that goal is reached? For example, take someone who's made it their life's goal to summit the tallest mountain in the world: Mt. Everest. Whereas in the United States, summiting Everest might be seen primarily as a personal achievement and a story to brag about (and rightly so), in other countries, reaching the summit can lead to instant fame; some governments even grant successful climbers property and monetary prizes. A singular focus on such a monumental task, like summiting Everest, can put tremendous pressure on an individual. It can create a sense that one's entire identity and worth are tied to this single achievement, leading to intense stress and anxiety, especially if there are signs of failure or difficulty.

We must remind ourselves that life doesn't end after achieving one goal; there's always a next step or another mountain to climb. Knowing there's another goal waiting for us fuels our drive to succeed and fosters persistence, even when the path gets tough. Learning to listen to those callings and understand when they are trying to distract us or when they are helping us make the most out of this one life is critical to becoming breakproof every step along the way.

When I reached the top of Mt. Tyree, I took a minute to look at the landscape and what I'd achieved. Only then did I focus on what was next, allowing myself to be both grateful looking back and hopeful looking forward. I relished my achievement, but another mountain was already calling me forth. Descending Mt. Tyree wasn't just a return journey; it was a continuation of the adventure. With every step down, I carried the lessons, experiences, and memories from the climb, invaluable assets for my next journey—another mountain or a different kind of adventure altogether.

This is a lesson not just for climbing but for life. Keep your vision clear on the step in front of you, but never lose sight of the endless possibilities that lie beyond.

// REFLECTION QUESTIONS

1. Consider a significant personal or professional goal. How does
   your vision of this goal change with different perspectives? What
   specific actions or steps might you be overlooking when you
   focus only on the big picture of your goal? How can focusing
   too much on small details cause you to lose sight of your
   overall objective?

   _____

   _____

   _____

   _____

   _____

   _____

2. What are the "blue ice" moments you're currently facing where
   increased effort simply won't take hold and move you forward?
   What strategies can you employ to overcome these challenges
   and progress toward your goal?

   _____

   _____

   _____

   _____

   _____

CHAPTER 2

FULLY COMMIT OR DON'T CLIMB THE MOUNTAIN

MT. LOGAN

In mountaineering, the journey often oscillates between two geographical extremes. After summiting Mt. Tyree in Antarctica, the southernmost of the Seven Second Summits, I attempted the northernmost peak: Mt. Logan, located on the border between Alaska and Canada's Yukon Territory.

Mt. Logan, named after Sir William Edmond Logan, a renowned Canadian geologist, is the highest peak in Canada and the second highest in North America. While its altitude is impressive, what truly makes this mountain significant is its unique geological feature: Mt. Logan is constantly growing due to active tectonic uplifting. Historical climbs have resulted in both triumph and tragedy, reflecting the mountain's unpredictable nature. The combination of geography and history diametrically amplifies the challenge and allure of this climb.

Among the Seven Second Summits, Mt. Tyree and Mt. Logan have striking similarities: during their respective climbing seasons, the sun never truly sets—it might dip behind mountains, lending a brief illusion of dusk, but true darkness never takes hold; both experience extreme weather patterns; and both are profoundly cold (not that any of the Second Summits are particularly *warm*). I hired a familiar face, Todd Passey, an experienced IFMGA mountain guide specializing in wilderness expeditions and survival training, who had previously guided me up Mt. Tyree and was my anchor during the Mt. Logan adventure.

Todd, Seba (another guide), and I had shared the thrill of summiting Tyree together, which had formed a strong bond of trust between us. We needed one more guide, so Todd's long-climbing partner also joined us. Sandro, my friend and videographer, joined along with two other clients from Australia. Together, our small band faced one of the most challenging climbs open to mountaineers. And it would prove more difficult than we imagined.

Quitting is when you give up on yourself because you no longer believe you're capable.

I'm going to break some hard news to you first: I didn't summit Mt. Logan on my first attempt. I know, for a book called *BreakProof* that's all about resiliency in the face of long odds, there sure seems to be a lot of perceived "breaking" and quitting involved. But for any ambitious goal, the journey to success isn't always straightforward. And even though my first attempt didn't deliver the desired result, I learned so much about not quitting from Mt. Logan that I summited a year later on my second attempt. I became more resilient and breakproof.

Much of popular psychology encourages us never to quit. Quitters are losers. Double down and keep going. Suck it up and show no weakness. But my experience on Mt. Logan prompted a deeper reflection on the nature of quitting and what it means, which I've come to understand may be different for me than it is for you. Remember, my definition of quitting is *to no longer expand or grow*. Sometimes you need to stop. Sometimes you need to end. Sometimes you're finished before the finish line you initially set for yourself. Sometimes the knowledge you've gained has caused you to pivot and pursue a different path. Setbacks, tragedies, and failures will always present themselves as opportunities to redefine your success. That redefinition doesn't necessarily mean you've quit. Quitting is when you give up on yourself because you no longer believe you're capable.

I host a podcast called *Seek Your Summit*, where I recently interviewed a guest who serves as a professional ghostwriter for people in the midst of trauma therapy. Part of their therapeutic process is writing a book, but not one in the traditional sense—not one you'll see on the shelf in Barnes & Noble. Their book will never be published in print, digital, or audio. Their "summit" is processing the trauma through writing their story. For most, writing a book and never publishing it might be considered quitting, but in this example, publishing was never their definition of success.

Sometimes, stopping a pursuit is viewed as quitting; however, in many cases, it's a redirection of energy and purpose. This redirection can be due to a realization that the goal was not aligned with one's authentic self or that circumstances and desires have changed. It is essential to differentiate between giving up on a goal due to a lack of belief in oneself (quitting), and making a conscious, intentional shift in direction. I know people whose parents think they quit graduate school, but in fact, they simply stopped. It turned out to be the wrong summit for them, and they chose not to waste their precious time and energy on something that would be meaningless in their life. There was a time when I played college soccer, and I stopped (perhaps viewed by some on the team as quitting). I didn't quit. I stopped. I realized early on that my goal wasn't to become a professional soccer player. We all know people that have ended relationships, closed businesses, and transitioned out of careers or industries. That doesn't mean they quit. When you combine wisdom with intentionality and a connection to purpose and end an effort, that's not quitting.

Becoming breakproof requires that you stay in your power, which may mean pausing, reassessing, and redefining your next step forward against a new meaningful goal with integrated intelligence. That's a fancy phrase: integrated intelligence. It means checking in with yourself by combining your unique experience, knowledge, and perhaps recalibrated desires to ensure you're living your authentic life—that the goals you're setting for yourself are worthy of accomplishing, and that you're not setting yourself up for breaking or quitting. Because sometimes you set yourself up to quit things you shouldn't have been doing in the first place.

In essence, the way you define quitting shapes your journey. For me, becoming breakproof revolves around one question: Am I still growing and expanding? If not, I'm quitting; if so, I'm on the right path.

The First Ascent

The periods between my mountain ascents, like the one after Mt. Tyree, were reserved for my children. As their laughter filled our home during pancake breakfasts and movie nights, I was reminded of why I climb: to show them the importance of chasing one's dreams. Being a mother of seven, I don't get much time to myself, but whenever I'm without my kids, I constantly think of them. I returned home from Antarctica in January and didn't have to be in Canada until May, so I took full advantage of those months in between.

Still, I had to prepare. Nestled in the heart of the Saint Elias Mountain Range that straddles Alaska and Canada, Mt. Logan stands at 5,956 meters (19,551 feet). Every step on Mt. Logan was a calculated risk, the cold wind biting at my face as I navigated this frozen, treacherous landscape; the snow beneath my boots potentially concealing a hidden, lethal crevasse—a gaping mouth ready to swallow climbers whole. It made the ascent not just about physical endurance but also mental fortitude. A formidable challenge to say the least. It also exacerbated a reality found on the other Second Summits: that given its lack of popularity, there weren't minimal support services; there were none. You fly a plane to the side of the mountain, it leaves, and you'd be lucky if you ran into another climbing team your entire expedition. It's a desolate, humanless terrain. For comparison, Mt. Denali (the highest peak in North America) issues around fifteen hundred permits each climbing season to athletes hoping to summit.

How many permits are issued for Mt. Logan each season? Maybe twenty. Thirty in a good year.

With a scarcity of fellow climbers and an unforgiving terrain, I knew I had to be ready for anything. On some of the Second Summits, mountaineering rules allow porters to support your efforts by carrying a portion of your gear. Mt. Logan forbids the use of porters, and as a mother of seven used to juggling daily life, I found myself faced with a different kind of balancing act. Typically, climbers often bear loads equal to 60 to 80 percent of their body weight, and this time was no exception. I had to carry my entire pack, a staggering 80 pounds—a weight that included group gear and was somewhat alleviated by my use of a sled. The first year, with a larger team, I had the luxury of distributing the weight more evenly among team members, carrying a lighter pack. However, during the second year, with only three of us, the burden grew substantially. But remember, I'm breakproof. The weight of my gear was the least of my challenges.

Carry All Your Gear

Here's a little fact that may surprise you: climbers don't always carry all their gear. For some mountains, you'll have your base camp at the bottom and anywhere between one and five additional camps at different intervals up the mountain. Mt. Logan had six camps (one base camp and five potential additional camps along the way). For more popular mountains, porters may have set up all of those campsites in advance. Sometimes they'll even bring food and other supplies up for you, so the only gear you're carting up and down the mountain are the bare necessities.

However, when climbing a less-frequented mountain, you must set up camp at each site entirely by yourself. Which means you have to carry all your gear with you.

No sweat! That's why people invented sleds. Well, that's not *why* people invented sleds. Some people use them for fun. Don't I wish that was my intended use of said sled. And just as in the everyday world, getting ahead is about working smarter, not harder. Rather than carry everything on my back, I packed most of my gear on a sled and skied up the side of the mountain, tugging all my gear behind me. Yes, I said I skied *up* a mountain. Also not why people invented skis. But remember, I'm breakproof.

Here's the main challenge: When you're responsible for carrying all your gear, you spend most of the climb shuttling equipment up and down the mountainside. Each morning was an arduous start, weighed down by not only our personal gear but the added equipment needed to set up camp at each new site. It was a never-ending cycle of hauling, unpacking, packing, and hauling again—a relentless test of strength, endurance, and determination. It was a perpetual cycle of physical exertion and mental fatigue. Not to mention freezing cold weather, as most days the temperature hovered around -30°F for two and a half weeks. This is like living outside in Fargo, North Dakota, in the winter for twenty days with your life on your back and a sled. Here's the long-winded breakdown:

Step 1: Arrive at Mt. Logan base camp with my tent, snow gear, sleeping gear, food, etc.

Step 2: Carry all the gear necessary for Camp 1 up to its location.

Step 3: *Bury all my gear.* I'm not kidding. You don't even get to spend the night at Camp 1. It takes so long, and the weather is so fickle that it's unsafe to ski to Camp 1 and set it up on the same day.

Step 4: Ski back down to base camp and go to sleep.

Step 5: Wake up and ski up to Camp 1 as fast as possible with the rest of your gear and tents.

Step 6: Adapt your camp setup based on your team size and mission demands. On our first year on Mt. Logan, with a larger team of seven members, we established a camp that included three sleeping tents and one larger dining tent to accommodate everyone during mealtimes. Given the size of the group, it was necessary to have this dining tent, as no individual tent was large enough for all of us to cook and eat in comfortably. However, during the second ascent, our team was trimmed down to just three. This meant we utilized a single, more spacious four-man tent for all purposes, even crafting a vestibule by digging out a section for cooking. Opting for three people was a strategic decision; a fourth would require a second tent, increasing our workload without significantly enhancing our advantages.

After setting up the tents, it's vital to dig up and organize the stored gear, ensuring everything needed is accessible and ready for use.

Next, we tackle the challenge of wind walls. On Mt. Logan, you must grapple with the dual challenges of whipping winds and relentless snowfalls, although they don't typically present simultaneously. In order to make sure you can sleep safely and your tents don't get torn to shreds by the wind, you have to set up wind walls. You must dig up igloo blocks to form these wind walls around your tents. And in case you're wondering, there aren't already formed nice blocks of ice that you watched in the Chilly Willy cartoons as he made his igloo. We packed saws with us to cut hundreds of our own igloo blocks at every camp, about the size of a concrete cinder block. Cutting, stacking, building; cutting, stacking, building until we had made a life-saving barrier around our tent.

Between setting up tents and building wind walls, it takes about four hours to set up camp *if you're lucky*. But you must do it right to fend off the elements, or you're in grave danger. So much hinges on the fragile fabric of your tent. A misstep leading to a destroyed tent doesn't just mean inconvenience; it signals the premature end of the expedition. Lousy weather is annoying enough *off* a mountain; it's a nightmare *on* one.

Step 7: Go to sleep at Camp 1.

Step 8: Carry your gear up to Camp 2 and repeat the inchworming process—moving up and down the mountainside to transport gear—all over again.

Such is the detailed, strenuous process of transporting gear up Mt. Logan. By the time you reach the summit, you've walked the entire length of the trail two or three times. That's 60 to 90 kilometers (37 to 56 miles) of climbing. If conditions are perfect, you can summit and descend in two weeks. If conditions aren't ideal, double it.

On our first attempt, our climb was fraught with challenges. Our initial days were marked by setbacks—conditions, far from ideal, began to test our resilience and unity as a team. The airplane that was supposed to fly us to Mt. Logan was broken, so we were delayed getting to the glacier by several days, waiting for parts to come in. Frigid temperatures were causing our days to be a bit slower, waiting for the sun to partially rise so we could safely progress up the mountain. We experienced storms here and there along the way for the first few days, though none threatened the climb. Luckily, our wind walls held up, and whenever we had close to clear skies, we would begin our inchworming process over again.

Yet, we ran into other challenges. Once we made it to Camp 2, Todd got sick. In our everyday lives, getting sick might mean a quick trip to a pharmacy and a day or two off of work; but on a mountain, even the common cold can quickly progress into something much more life-threatening. Todd and Tim returned to Camp 1 to see if the lower elevation would help Todd recover. The rest of us stayed at Camp 2 for a few extra days. Todd didn't get better, so it was time to split the team. Todd and the Australians went down, while the rest of us, with heavy hearts, had to decide whether to continue or abort the mission.

We continued.

The meticulous inchworming process and our extensive safety checks may seem tedious to an outsider. But in the unpredictable world of high-altitude climbing, this attention to detail is far from an exaggeration; it's a lifesaving discipline. Safety comes first when climbing (and in life), particularly when you can't even trust the ground you walk on, for it can split into a crevasse at any moment.

If you think inchworming sounds like a waste of time and a tedious process in the name of safety, just wait until I introduce you to the wonders of *skiing* up the mountain.

For Safety, Double- and Triple-Check (or How to Avoid Crevasses)

Every mountain has its perils, but Mt. Logan isn't just a mountain. By that, I mean it's not just a jagged stack of rocks coming out of the ground. Mt. Logan is a glacier—eons-old ice with large crevasses between its slick ridges. The biggest threats on Mt. Logan are those crevasses—deep, open cracks in the glacier ice. These crevasses form as the glacier moves and stretches, and they can be wide, deep, and often hidden by fresh snow, making them an insidious risk for climbers. Skiing on ice is scary enough, but when ice splitting means falling hundreds of feet to your inevitable death, you will start watching where you step—carefully, watching... each... step—every placement of every forward movement.

Sometimes, the best solution is the simplest one.

To make the ascent as safe as possible, we used a high-tech, ultraintelligent technique that's been a trade secret for decades: poke the ice with a stick.

Sometimes, the best solution is the simplest one.

Every step we took up the mountain comprised a three-step (poke) process. Because we were skiing up the mountain with an entire camp in a sled behind us, the expedition leader always had ski poles. These came in handy for checking the ground before us for loose ice or snow that might be hiding a crevasse beneath it (or be slick enough to send us over the side). Painstakingly, our guide would poke the ice to the left, poke in the middle, and poke on the right—tens of thousands of times. So long as the ice didn't give out from that pressure, we were safe to take *one ski step forward*.

Climbing mountains has taught me to be patient. It's not the first word that comes to mind when people described me before my mountaineering expedition. Still, it's a practice and competency I developed out of necessity that I've now learned to better leverage in my life off the mountain in my most important roles as parent, friend, and entrepreneur. I'm not exactly reckless, but my default mindset is to believe that anything is possible. More specifically, I *don't* think anything is *impossible*. So my drive to succeed against impossible odds manifests as something others might call impatience. But when I saw a seasoned sherpa on Mt. Everest unclip from the rope to take a few steps to the side to relieve himself, only to tragically fall into a crevasse, it served as a stark reminder of the relentless and unforgiving nature of the mountains. It was a poignant lesson in patience and respect for our environment.

Being patient and deliberate was key on Mt. Logan. It could have been very easy for me to skip all of the safety checks or try to carry more up than I could manage, but I cured that temptation with one of my strengths: I have a knack for making even the most mundane tasks a game. Were we excited to check the path in front of me three times for every step? Not necessarily. I was making progress, which was exciting enough to keep me on track. But looking back at my trail, I noticed that the scratches I left behind looked like little stitches. To keep myself focused and patient during this repetitive but critical task, I visualized each poke of the ski pole as a suture in a delicate surgical procedure, each step methodically closing the gap between me and the summit. This may seem hokey, but I have found this to be instrumental in my quest to exercise necessary patience when my natural proclivity tends toward impatience.

The journey from Camp 3 to Camp 4 on Mt. Logan presents a peculiar challenge. Both camps are situated at approximately 16,000 feet, with a deceptive mini mountain lying between the two. To move from Camp 3 to Camp 4, climbers must first ascend to a height of 18,100 feet and then descend back to 16,000 feet to reach Camp 4. Recognizing the exhausting nature of this yo-yo climb, our team made a strategic choice. Instead of lugging our gear directly to Camp 4, we decided to deposit it at the peak of this mini mountain. By doing so, we figured that skiing down with our equipment the next day would be more efficient than enduring the up-and-down journey with full loads. As we huddled in our tents each night, the howling wind served as a stark reminder of the mountain's unforgiving nature. Every step thinned the air and intensified the cold, but our sights remained fixed on Camp 4, our last stop before the summit push. The skies stayed mostly clear, fueling our determination to reach the summit in the days ahead. I'd committed to this journey and would make it through thick ice and thin air.

At least, that was the plan.

Know Your Team's Strengths (and Weaknesses)

Getting up at sunrise becomes nebulous when the sun never *actually* rises. But adapting to unfamiliar and challenging circumstances is crucial to mountaineering and navigating life's complexities. In Antarctica, I dealt with perpetual noon; Canada was similar, although we did have about two hours of dawn from 2 to 4 a.m. every morning. Finally, the morning came when it was time to move to Camp 4.

I was tired but eager. I emerged from my tent as the rest of the team woke up and prepared for our final leg. As we were discussing our plans, we received incoming weather reports. We took a moment, analyzing the data and debating our options, waiting to see if conditions might improve. That was when Tim broke the news.

"The trip's over," Tim said.

I thought I misheard him. We all did. "What do you mean?" I said.

"The trip's over. We have to descend."

I was confused and frustrated. We were just two days from summiting. Why quit now? Was it the snow? The climbing season for Mt. Logan typically concludes at the end of June due to the onset of snowmelt.

Once that starts, crevasses become impassable, and climbing is too dangerous. But it was just the middle of May. We still had plenty of time left. Were we out of food? That couldn't be it. Unless someone had been secretly snacking every night, we should have had enough supplies to make it to the summit and back to base camp before running out of food. Even if that were the case, I was ready to ration food if necessary.

We were on course. How could everything have changed so drastically in a matter of minutes?

"A storm is expected to be coming in," Tim said. "It's going to delay us coming back down the mountain, and I can't afford that."

Seriously? A storm? We'd already been through several small storms; based on our data, this one wouldn't be half as bad. Okay, to be fair, we were expected to get temperatures as low as -65°F, and we were underequipped with ski boots, not rugged 8,000-meter climbing boots specially made for that kind of weather. Still, we'd weathered storms before. How could this be any worse?

And who cares about a little delay? The difference of a day or two when descending barely means anything in the grand scheme. Why throw away weeks of climbing because it bled a day or two into your schedule?

It turns out that the root of our disagreement was deeply personal and relatable: Tim had promised to be there for his child's kindergarten graduation, a milestone that held immense significance for him. He couldn't bear the thought of missing this precious moment in his child's life—a promise is a promise, especially to our kids. We had likely been too optimistic in our initial estimates of the time the climb would take, and given the unexpected delays we encountered, Tim was faced with a heart-wrenching decision: to call off the climb. Ultimately, his commitment to his family prevailed, making him unwilling to continue. Maybe we could have overruled him, outvoted him, and pushed on despite his concerns, but that would have violated the unspoken code of mountaineering: no one gets left behind, and no one gets left out. Clearly, this was a time when I was confronted with my governing value of "people over peaks." Talk about exercising integrity at a critical moment of choice. I wanted to push on and was immensely frustrated at Tim's surprise announcement. But as much as it hurt, we had to respect his decision, even if it meant our dreams of reaching the summit would have to wait. I respected his devotion to his family, and when you're on a team, you don't move forward unless everyone is comfortable moving forward. And you don't let someone descend the mountain alone. Your team is your most important asset on a mountain and in everyday life. Since Tim was done, we were all done. There we were, so close to the summit, the culmination of our shared sacrifices within reach, and in the final stretch, we had to turn back. I can't blame Tim for calling it quits when he did, but to say my hopes were dashed with that decision would be a colossal understatement.

A key lesson I learned was ensuring everyone commits to the commitment and openly discusses where their limitations lie and what might result in breaking their commitment. In this case, it was a calendaring issue—a stark reminder of how our priorities can dramatically impact those around us. I realized then that mountaineering is more than just a physical climb; it's about team dynamics, understanding, and respecting each other's boundaries. It's also about clarifying your own and making sure everyone understands them and is comfortable accommodating them, even if it hijacks the goal. It's about recognizing that reaching the summit is not always the measure of success. Reaching the summit *together* is.

I broke inside like falling ice. It felt like my dreams were vanishing into the thin alpine air. My hopes so fervently nurtured—often under harsh circumstances—seemed to be unraveling in front of my eyes. I was crushed because of what it would take to climb this mountain again. A few extra days pushing forward was tiny compared to future training and time away from home and enduring this mountain again. Not to mention the financial investment it would take to assemble this expedition again. I'd wanted to set an example for my kids. I was doing this as much for them as much as I was for myself. In fact, I was doing this for them *more* than I was for myself.

Mom can do hard things, *borderline impossible* things, and so can you.

But… people over peaks.

You don't go on without your team.

We skied up to Camp 4 (I know, still an odd concept that you ski *up*), gathered our stuff, and descended the mountain. It felt like a walk of shame. If I'd been in any mood to joke, I would have called it a ski of shame. That kind of humor only feels funny in hindsight, though.

This was one of many true tests of being breakproof. Instead of wallowing in the disappointment, I chose to use this setback as a reminder of my resilience, a testament to the fact that I could, and would, return to face this mountain, next time with a team that was vetted for commitment to the commitment. As we descended, a deep sense of disappointment washed over me. The realization that I had come within touching distance of—and yet remained so far from—success was the bitter pill I reluctantly swallowed for a twelve-plus hour journey down the mountain. But that bitterness flashed into a spark inside my gut.

> **Knowing a team's strengths and weaknesses is more than strategy; it's about empathy, respect, and shared commitment.**

As we descended, I understood that knowing a team's strengths and weaknesses is more than strategy; it's about empathy, respect, and shared commitment. Next time, I would be ready, and so would my team. This setback wasn't the end; it was merely a detour. I couldn't be broken that easily. We had stopped, not quit. After all, I was becoming breakproof.

The Second Ascent

Mt. Logan ultimately became the seventh and concluding milestone in my quest to conquer the Seven Second Summits. By the time the season had opened again, I'd successfully summited Mt. Townsend in Australia, and took a second successful swing at K2, both of which came with their own hurdles to leap over. But those are stories for other chapters.

Having gone through my fair share of challenging climbs and equipped with valuable experience and knowledge from my first attempt, I knew I couldn't delay any longer. One way or another, I was going to summit Mt. Logan.

Commitment Makes You Stronger

From Day One of my second attempt at Mt. Logan, I knew things would be different. Todd joined again for this climb, as did a friend of mine named Ryan, whom I'd climbed with before and trusted to the ends of the earth. It turns out that's precisely where I took him.

I'm tempted to say those first few days were easier, but that wouldn't be accurate. It's better to say that I climbed the mountain more easily. The difference may seem like splitting hairs, but it's an important distinction. The difference was in me: I climbed more confidently and efficiently this time. Climbing from base camp to Camp 1 took roughly the same time, but I knew what I was doing. I could anticipate which sections would be more complex and when would be a good time to rest. Yes, the terrain had changed from one year to the next, but that first stretch was relatively the same. And having walked the path before, I could mentally prepare more effectively. When there are fewer unknowns, I don't have to spend mental energy hyping myself up, and that spare energy can instead be marshaled toward the physical stresses of climbing.

Even with the extra mental energy, we still had to be mindful of our physical fuel. When it comes to climbing, you don't get a second chance if you run out of food.

Stay Fueled

Most athletic feats come with a guarantee of weight loss. On average, a marathon runner will lose around 6 to 10 pounds between Mile 0 and the finish line. Football padding isn't designed around ventilation, meaning a player can lose over 5 pounds of water during a game. And NASCAR drivers endure temperatures of up to and beyond 100°F, and even when constantly hydrating, they can lose 5 to 10 pounds in one race. Therefore, one might assume I'd lose weight while climbing a mountain due to intense calorie burn over several weeks. But the truth is, I stayed about the same weight on most of my climbs. I actually *gained* weight on Mt. Logan. How? I stayed fueled by consuming high-calorie, nutrient-packed meals like energy bars, protein-rich stews, and carb-loaded pasta. These meals, designed to fuel our strenuous climb and combat the cold, prevented significant weight loss despite intense physical exertion, and also had a surprising side effect: a few extra pounds. Yes, I was spending tons of energy, but most of that energy was spent keeping myself warm. When I looked at balancing my energy intake and output, I realized that if I ever came up short, I could go into hypothermia or end up with frostbite. It only takes one missed meal to send your energy plummeting, leaving you weak, disoriented, and far more vulnerable to the elements. And because I wasn't willing to risk that, I kept myself energized enough that weight loss didn't become a problem.

When climbing mountains, I always took careful note of just how much food I was consuming and how much energy I was expending. While we were aggressive in our ascent plans, we always ensured that we had reserves of food to fall back on. If I didn't provide my body with enough energy, I risked much more than fatigue; I faced the threats of severe dehydration, impaired judgment due to low energy, and an increased susceptibility to the harsh elements, which could all jeopardize the entire expedition. If a runner gets a cramp in their calf halfway through a race, that's unfortunate, but they're no more than three minutes from a trainer who can attend to their needs. Within ten minutes, they've been hydrated, pumped full of electrolytes, and have finished off their granola bar or orange slices. They've lost a race, but otherwise, they're fine. On the other hand, if I'm two-thirds of the way up a mountain with crevasses on either side of me (and potentially one directly beneath me) with limited radio and GPS signal and no more than half-a-dozen people within 20 miles of my location on the largest mountain by land mass in the world, and *then* I get a cramp? I'm not just risking my ability to summit; I'm risking my life and the lives of my teammates. People over peaks.

While the remoteness of Mt. Logan doesn't compare to that of Antarctica, where isolation took on a new, chilling meaning, I wasn't taking any chances. I was determined not to gamble with my health, having learned hard lessons from my icy days on the southernmost continent. I made sure I was eating whenever possible and constantly checking in on Todd and Ryan to do the same. And they were just as vigilant with me. None of us were willing to jeopardize our summit attempt, and potentially our lives, for something as mundane as tummy troubles. We meticulously planned our meals and monitored our bodies to avoid nutrition-related issues.

Because we were vigilant and experienced, we were making great time. By the time we'd reached Camp 2, we were on pace to set the record for the fastest-known time for summiting. And because we had to carry everything up the mountain, we brought only the minimum necessary food to Camp 3. Given our pace and previous experience, but as an extra safety margin, we budgeted for a total of seven days worth of food in order to reach the summit and return safely. This calculation was based on our detailed daily energy-expenditure estimates and our desire to strike a balance between carrying weight and ensuring adequate nutrition. If all went well, we wouldn't need more than what we brought.

Of course, rarely does everything go according to plan. And we were about to find this out the hard way.

The Right People Fight Hardest

Remember what I said about Mt. Logan's weather—how you either endure the snow or stand firm against the wind, but rarely both? You guessed it. We got both. The biting wind threatened to knock us off our feet, and snow blurred our vision until we couldn't distinguish sky from ground.

We had just finished setting up Camp 3 when the weather report came in. Since we were higher up the mountain, we pulled weather forecasts from numerous reports to compare and make the smartest decisions based on those readings. Usually, most reports would skew one way, and one or two would report different findings and skew another. Rarely would we get a unanimous report, so we would discuss the likelihood of each report being accurate and decide whether to climb or wait based on the collective forecasts for that day. When we woke up at Camp 3, we got as close to a unanimous report as we'd ever received on the mountain, and it wasn't good.

The directive was clear: Stay put.

I retreated to our tent, brushing snow off the big igloo-block wind wall we'd built on one side, and I could feel the icy air biting at my cheeks as I closed my eyes and prayed for the best. So far, the climb had been a textbook situation. It was better than textbook. Thinking back to my first attempt, we were a mess when we made it to Camp 2. This year, we were at Camp 3 and sitting strong. The weather had been forgiving, and the team had high hopes. Now it seemed our luck had run out.

To be clear, the climb was still arduous. There's no easy way up a mountain. But even when the path forward became difficult, we'd all made a silent agreement not to complain. If any one of us voiced dissatisfaction, we knew the rest would join in, and before we knew it, our descent in morale would result in a physical descent back to base camp. We'd been successful thus far, but a storm like this could break us. And we all knew it.

The storm kept us at Camp 3 for a full week, but the worst of it lasted for a solid fourteen hours. During that time, I endured the most brutal weather this mountain had to offer. We had no visibility and had to set markers, even when relieving ourselves. That's how disorienting a storm like this can be.

Hunkered down in our tent, hoping our wind walls worked like they were meant to, we sat, waited, and prayed. Admitting fear would be an understatement. Honestly, this was the most terrified I'd felt on any mountain that year. As the storm roared around our tiny camp, each gust threatened to rip our tents from the frozen ground. I felt a fear that was both bone-chilling and mind-numbing, the kind of fear that makes you question not just your decisions but your sanity. What was I even doing on this mountain? Why would I brave these horrendous conditions in the first place? What could I possibly get out of this? Becoming breakproof requires a sometimes continuous reconnection to your purpose and mission, especially amid adversity. In this case, my "adversity" was either being blown off the mountain or becoming a frozen statue of myself—a dead one.

Some storms will delay a climb. That's not too out of the ordinary. You can plan around that. Other storms, however, end a climb. This one threatened to be the latter. As the wind howled outside our tent, I lay wide awake. The uncertainty of our situation and the storm that seemed to never end triggered a wave of anxiety. I wish I could say my ironclad resolve—the unshakeable commitment I had made to myself to summit, not to quit—remained unwavering beneath it all, but my resiliency was fading. When you're on the mountain with nothing between you and the ravages of Mother Nature, you have to consider your situation. You want to achieve your goals, but no goal is worth your life. Let me repeat that: *No goal is worth your life.* No summit, no achievement, no accolade is worth the price of the rest of your future. This is a gentle but vital reminder to prioritize your well-being and safety in life's pursuits.

To make matters worse, because the snow and wind conspired together, our wind wall became a snow-accumulation wall, threatening to bury our tent entirely. For this second attempt, we'd all slept in the same tent, which proved to be a godsend for surviving the storm. Enduring something this fierce alone would have been maddening. Not to mention, it meant we could divide up the labor. Many hands, as the saying goes. Every two or three hours, we had to emerge from our shelter and unbury the tent as best we could, braving the cold before slipping back inside.

And when I say unbury, I mean excavate. Every time we opened the tent flap, we were completely buried in the snow, so we had to dig a hole up and out to get to air, only to be bombarded by cold daggers of wind. It was the kind of sharp cold that could kill. If our tent ripped, I knew we were as good as dead. At some point in the middle of this storm, I couldn't help but think, "Wow. Is this some weird twist to the end of my life?"

But I fought. We all fought. Initially, our plan was to go from Camp 2 directly to Camp 4, bypassing Camp 3. However, as we reached the Camp 3 area, we realized why Camp 3 was advertised as a necessary stop: we were exhausted. In addition, visibility is paramount on this mountain, both for safety and to maintain a sense of direction—poor visibility made it impossible to proceed safely. We ran into another group from Austria and decided to set up camp and not go all the way to Camp 4.

As a storm threatened to hit, both teams were stuck at Camp 3, so we strategized together: We would stay put until the weather improved and make Tuesday our day to push from Camp 3 to the summit, passing the other camps. A grueling fourteen-hour ordeal followed, during which a violent storm held both teams hostage, and we genuinely believed we might not survive.

When the storm ceased, the bad visibility persisted. By the time the sun finally graced us with its presence on Sunday evening, our food reserves had dwindled to a mere two days' worth. So on that Sunday night, we decided to descend for more supplies. Descending became not just an option but a necessity, though the storm had eradicated our tracks, making each step challenging. Luckily, we didn't have to descend to base camp because we had left emergency supplies and another tent at Camp 2, saving us several days of travel. The plan was to refuel and turn around to head back to Camp 3 without delay, catching up to the Austrians the following day, Monday. We could still make good time.

But on that Sunday, Ryan got frostbite.

His fingers were numb, and he knew as well as we did what that meant. Even though you get roughly the same amount of sunlight throughout the day, there are still temperature drops late at night when the sun dips below the horizon. And 2 a.m. is as cold as it gets, between -40 and -50°. Although there are multiple contributors to frostbite (inadequate hydration, extreme temperatures, reduced blood flow, etc.), Ryan's fingers had been exposed to the just-too-cold air for just too long. Our push to the summit became a push to get Ryan to safety. We had to get him off the mountain. People over peaks.

We contacted park officials and Global Rescue. A helicopter evacuation was impossible, due to the poor weather, but there was hope for Tuesday. Todd and I worked to keep Ryan safe and medically stable, fighting against time to avoid amputation—a real possibility. Meanwhile, our Austrian companions at Camp 3 pressed on toward the summit on Tuesday without us.

This was among the longest days I've ever spent on a mountain, with every second spent fighting frostbite's chilling clutches. But Ryan, despite his pain, encouraged us to continue our ascent. The helicopter only had room for one person, so Todd and I would be left on the mountainside with our summit dreams still alive. As we bid Ryan farewell, his optimism for us remained strong, despite our shared disappointment at not being able to summit together.

After Ryan was airlifted out that Tuesday, Todd and I wondered if we could catch up with the Austrians so we could all summit together. Things didn't go as planned, however. First, our ascent without Ryan proved laborious: He was the strongest member of our team; tall and fit, he could carry a lot more than I did. Second, to our surprise, the Austrians returned to our camp telling us they'd failed to summit. The Austrians advised that we should move to Camp 4 and make our summit push from there, arguing that the distance from Camp 3 to the summit was too great. So, on Wednesday, Todd and I headed to Camp 4.

In addition to their useful advice, the Austrians had left us another important gift: markers along the path to show the safest route, up as far as they'd gotten before their failed attempt. I was blessed again with others looking out for me even when their hopes had been dashed. We made it to Camp 4 that Wednesday without incident.

The next day, with clear skies and rock-hard determination, Todd and I climbed the last stretch to the peak. And all at once, at 3:30 p.m. Pacific Time, Thursday, June 1, 2023, I marked my place in history as not only the first American, but also the first woman ever to complete the Seven Second Summits.

But even more importantly, I demonstrated to each of my seven treasured children their ability to face challenges head-on, to become breakproof just like their mother. Standing on the peak, I realized that being breakproof was more than a mantra; it was a commitment to face life's storms head-on. It's a lesson I'd carry down from the mountain and into the rest of my life.

BE BREAKPROOF: HOW TO FULLY COMMIT TO YOUR MOUNTAIN

1. **Decide.** Much like climbing a mountain, achieving any significant goal requires a clear and unwavering commitment, as well as the determination to push forward, regardless of the obstacles and challenges encountered.

2. **Emphasize Preparedness and Self-Sufficiency.** Equip yourself with the necessary tools and knowledge to deal with unexpected obstacles. Learn to be self-reliant; this involves carrying your own load and navigating through unpredictable circumstances.

3. **Work Smart, Not Just Hard.** Utilize available resources such as expert advice, technology, and time-management strategies to make tasks more manageable and efficient. And remember: Safety measures, even if they seem tedious, should always come first, both in extreme situations like mountain climbing and daily life.

4. **Exercise Patience and Persistence.** Treat your journey as a slow, meticulous process, taking one step at a time and being patient with your progress.

5. **Remember to Care for Basic Needs.** Consistently nourish your body with healthy food, get adequate sleep, and set aside time for mental and physical rest, especially in challenging situations. Stay fueled! Your "fuel" might be regular exercise and a healthy diet for a physical challenge or meditation and self-care for emotional well-being, depending on the nature of your "climb." Stay nourished! In the journey to achieving your goals, keeping yourself physically, mentally, and emotionally fed is crucial. Ask yourself: Based on my goal, how will I deplete myself? What can I do to prevent it, and how can I resolve it when it happens? Commitment requires energy, so keep yourself energized and check your energy levels regularly.

6. **Display Resilience and Endurance in Difficult Times.** Being breakproof means bouncing back from disappointments with renewed determination and the strength to endure hardships without losing focus on your goals.

7. **Understand the Difference Between Failure and Quitting.** Recognize that setbacks and failures provide opportunities for growth and learning, enhancing your resilience. They are not a reason to quit. Also, know when to stop; understand that stopping is not equivalent to quitting. Sometimes a pursuit may need to be stopped if it no longer aligns with your goals.

8. **Reevaluate and Adjust Your Goals.** Regularly reassess your goals based on the insights and experiences you've gained. This isn't about quitting; it's about proactively adjusting your path to align with something more meaningful or suitable. Stay empowered and connected to your purpose. This might involve pausing, reassessing, and redefining your steps forward.

9. **Place People Over Goals.** The safety and well-being of team members should always be prioritized over reaching the end goal. Recognize when to pivot or let go of a goal when the risk becomes too high. Placing people over goals also entails maintaining communication and respect in team dynamics. Communication is vital in preventing misunderstandings, understanding team members' capacities, and respecting individual priorities, ensuring efficient delegation and teamwork.

10. **Maintain a Spirit of Humility and Gratitude.** Regularly acknowledge and express appreciation for the efforts of others, and remind yourself of the progress you have made, even in tough times. This mindset can help you navigate through challenges and emerge stronger.

COMMIT TO THE COMMITMENT

Commitment is the foundation of resiliency; resiliency is the bedrock of being breakproof. Commitment means acknowledging the potential bumps in the road yet confidently choosing to stay the course because you believe it leads to your destination. When you commit yourself to a goal—starting a new business, writing a book, or losing weight—you're promising to see it through to completion, even if you have to pause for a moment. Remember, pausing doesn't mean you're quitting.

Sometimes you've got to climb down to climb up.

As you climb your respective mountains, you'll face disappointments, discouragement, and even disasters. I can promise you that. Even if the stars align and your climb up is without incident, climbing is inherently tricky. It will take grit, determination, and a reality that sometimes you've got to climb down to climb up.

Your First Commitment Is to Safety

There's a thrill that comes with chasing after a dream. For some, the dangers ahead aren't a deterrent but are part of the ride. Whether you thrive on adrenaline or occasionally enjoy flirting with danger and dabbling with risk, it's vital to prioritize safety above all—emotional safety, ensuring your mental well-being remains a priority; physical safety, taking steps to protect your body and health; cultural safety, being mindful of and respectful toward different cultures and environments, etc. Hardship and danger will come whether you ask for it or not, so *plan for it.*

When climbing Mt. Logan, my team and I were hemmed in by crevasses almost all day, every day. Whenever I dared to glance into the crevasse-ridden abyss, the thrill in my chest reminded me to take calculated steps. At the risk of becoming annoying, I'll repeat: People over peaks. And in many cases, when I say "people," I mean my small people back at our home in Utah. Ever-present in my mind was to prevent becoming a memory to my children and instead to become a model.

Starting a business might result in financial losses; learning a musical instrument and failing might feel like a waste of time; and training for a marathon only to never cross the finish line might bruise your ego. While your goal might not involve risking your life, my experiences on Mt. Logan—fraught with physical danger—can still inform your commitment to safety.

The first step is knowing exactly what your risks are. In my case, yawning crevasses flanked the mountain path. Avoiding them was as simple as not venturing too close to the edge. In your case, think about obvious solutions to obvious risks. For instance, if you are starting a business, a significant risk might be financial instability—your "crevasse." A simple step back from the edge might mean setting a strict budget and saving a portion of your income as a cushion before you dive into full-time entrepreneurship. Or, if you are training for a marathon, overexerting yourself could be your "crevasse." To stay safe, you might establish a training regimen that gradually increases in intensity, allowing your body to adapt without significant injury risk. Just as I had to be mindful of each step in a dangerous environment, you, too, must navigate your path with awareness and precaution, mitigating risks as you work toward your goals.

The truth is that it's rarely the risks we plan for that take us down, but it is often the net we build that saves us.

While it's crucial to be mindful of obvious risks, what about the ones that aren't blatantly obvious or that you couldn't foresee? These hidden or lurking dangers are just as critical to prepare for. The truth is that it's rarely the risks we plan for that take us down, but it is often the net we build that saves us. A storm will always be ahead, and you must weather the unforeseeable. Having the ability to absorb its effects plays a larger role in your success than planning for every possible hiccup that may come your way. Yes, we would all like to be in more control of our situation, but if you and I are honest with ourselves, there's more luck involved—good and bad—in our journey than we'd like to admit. Preparing a safety net—such as savings for financial downturns, a mentor for guidance, or a wellness routine for health—is what helps you absorb lousy luck and stay resilient.

On Mt. Logan, to uncover lurking risks, including crevasses, my team had to do our research before ever setting foot at the base of the mountain; we looked up stories of those who had successfully summited before us, hired guides who had experience in similar situations, and talked to experts. As an established entrepreneur and a member of a large business community, I can't stress enough the importance of thorough research before embarking on a new venture. I'm always surprised at how few well-educated business leaders and entrepreneurs take the time to do their research upfront—to invest in talking with people who have expeditioned ahead of them. There are always experts and people with greater insight in your field. Don't take that first step blind! Reach out, sign up for classes, or go to a convention. If you're chasing a goal on a budget, most experts have information online for free. (Make sure the information you're gathering is reliable. Verify the credibility of the sources and look for expert credentials or peer-reviewed information.)

Another risk we had to prepare for was the temperamental weather that threatened to bury us or blow us off the side of the mountain. On Mt. Logan, we used various GPS and weather-monitoring devices to get in-the-moment weather updates. Even when faced with conflicting reports, our guides were able to zero in on the best data that allowed us to make an informed decision. This data was a game changer when we were abruptly assailed by a maelstrom of wind and snow all at once. Without the extra time to secure our gear and tents, we could have faced a deadly storm with little preparation.

Just as we used up-to-date information to combat the elements on Mt. Logan, in your venture, staying informed with the most recent and reliable data is essential. This data helps you adapt and make informed decisions in a fluid environment. If you're starting a business, knowing the state of the macro and micro economy is paramount. How are other similar businesses performing in the current climate? What specific economic indicators should you be tracking that have a bearing on your endeavor? It may be the overall stock market or how federal interest rates affect banks and loans. It may be measures closer to home—for instance, whether there is a busy and slow season for your business—and if so, when do they occur, and how should your cash flow be managed accordingly? Preparing a safety net of information and knowledge will help you weather the storms. Find your goal's "GPS"—the tools and metrics that guide you toward your objectives— and your "weather service"—the sources that help you anticipate and prepare for potential challenges. Determine which resources will best suit your journey toward success.

Prioritize your safety, whether that means financial security, emotional well-being, or trusting reliable partners. You can't always predict a storm, but you can prepare for it.

Surround Yourself With Diehards

You may remember that my first summit attempt at Mt. Logan ended in disappointment. You may also recall that it wasn't my decision.

No matter your goal, it will take more than your individual efforts to get there. From teachers and mentors to those who provide moral and financial support, making your dreams a reality is a community effort. Consider pursuing your goal as akin to climbing a chain. Each link in the chain must be strong and secure if you're going to make it all the way up. When finding a community to help you, surround yourself with those who are just as committed as you are.

Easier said than done, right? Especially if achieving your dream, such as reaching a summit or starting a new business, takes you out of your comfort zone. Setting up connections can be intimidating and exhausting without a built-in community of friends and family already in the industry. In these instances, you may be tempted to rely on friends and associates who don't have any skin in the game and aren't interested in your endeavors or seeing them through to the end, and that can make achieving your goals even harder. So choose carefully.

To clarify, I am not suggesting that you abandon your family or that those who can't support you in your endeavors aren't genuinely your friends. They may have different ways of showing their support that are just as valid. Sometimes they won't support you from the start, and that's okay. They may not want to deal with the change. Stay strong; they may be more willing to come around with time and progress. Your current friends and family will likely support you in ways they know how. If you're launching a startup, they'll likely come to the launch event or refer potential clients to you. That is how they'll support you. But that's not the kind of support you'll need in the thick of it. That's where diehards come in.

Getting from where you are to where you need to go, you'll need people to support you, but you also need to recognize the different ways support manifests itself. If you relied on your friends to be present at every business meeting you have, you'd watch their flame of support dwindle and snuff out before you sign your first contract. That's not their fault. It's just not the support they're equipped to offer.

Who should be at your business meetings? Your business partners! If it's an investor pitch, other stakeholders and potential investors! Surround yourself with other entrepreneurs and business-minded individuals and rely on them for support throughout the startup journey. Doing so strengthens your commitment to your goals and increases your chance of achieving them.

Let me extend one last piece of advice in this section: No one will be as committed to your goal as you are. Expecting anyone to have an equal zeal as you will only end in disappointment and perhaps even conflict. You have to be the first person committed to your goal. However, if you surround yourself with people whose commitment to a goal matches yours, you can support each other. Sometimes that doesn't mean you match the kinds of goals you pursue but the intensity with which you pursue those goals.

Todd was (and continues to be) an incredible support in my mountaineering adventures. While he was only physically present for two of my summits, without his support and teachings, I wouldn't have made it up several of the mountains I've climbed. Todd isn't the first woman to complete the Seven Second Summits. I am, thanks to him and many others. But do you know what he will be? An expert mountaineer and guide who's scaled countless difficult mountains. That's his goal. And his goal and mine coexisted so well that neither of us was going to give up on the other. Because giving up on each other would mean giving up on ourselves.

When possible, create systems and provide opportunities for others to couple their goals with yours. Every time you do that, you increase your chances of accomplishing your goals and—as a bonus—help others along their path. You might not always be 100 percent in love with your goal, so having people to carry you is critical to success. They'll make up the difference while you recharge your commitment.

That's what it means to be committed to a goal; that's what it means to be part of a community. That's what it means to become breakproof.

Build Based on Strengths

Once you have your community, you'll discover an uncomfortable truth: people have weaknesses. Worse yet, *you* have weaknesses.

How can you make it up your mountain if you can't rely on your guides? If this guide can't manage their time well and your mentor has a poor sense of direction, how can you be confident in anyone? How can you have confidence in yourself?

Sorry to break it to you, nobody's perfect. There's no perfect entrepreneur, perfect musician, or perfect athlete.

But here's the thing: There never have been. And yet, businesses succeed, music is performed, and races are won. How is that possible? Because people chase their dreams based on their strengths, not their weaknesses.

Being part of a small team in a remote wilderness with limited supplies and little personal space, you quickly figure out people's weaknesses. Oddly enough, most of us are more adept at identifying flaws than recognizing strengths. For example, Todd was always willing to cook but burned more meals than any of us. Most of the time, everyone was grateful they could rest while Todd cooked, but we also had to keep an eye on him so we wouldn't eat charred remains. And we were able to pivot accordingly. Likewise, Ryan is a great climber but hesitated to voice his own needs. That may not matter in every instance, but when he got frostbite, he didn't want to tell us about it at first. Luckily, he spoke up when he knew it would put him and the rest of us in danger and we could get him to safety before things got too bad.

And you know what else? I could rely on both Todd and Ryan for moral support. Among their many skills and abilities, including their endurance and physical strength in braving some of the most challenging climbs on earth, they also maintained a positive attitude. And it was infectious.

When finding your community, build around others' strengths.

The truth is (and I'm sharing this publicly here for the first time), I considered quitting several times while climbing Mt. Logan. When the going gets tough, you can't help but wonder how nice it would be to just sleep in a regular bed. Forget memory-foam, pillow-topped, remote-controlled mattresses. Just a spring mattress in a cheap motel. That's the height of luxury when you're on a mountain 13,000 feet up, sleeping on a barely inflatable mattress pad with wind whipping so hard around you it feels like knives.

When I was weakest and wanted to turn around, Todd and Ryan kept my sights on the summit. Without their ability to keep me positive (without their strengths, despite their weaknesses), I would not have made it up Mt. Logan.

When finding your community, build around others' strengths. You know what you'll need to achieve your dream, and with a bit of introspection, you'll see where you're weakest. With more self-analysis, you'll know what will make you want to quit. Find people with the strengths that complement your weaknesses. Forget about their weaknesses, or better yet, use your strengths to help them! By doing so, you'll find your commitment less susceptible to buckling under pressure.

If at First You Don't Succeed, Learn

Failure is a common occurrence in life, an unfortunate reality. In pursuit of any goals, failures will pockmark the road before you. If you're lucky, you'll only come short once or twice on your way to ultimate success. No matter how often you're forced to turn around, however, becoming breakproof is about getting back on that mountain.

After failing to achieve your objective, regardless of what that may be, your most important next step is to reflect and learn. Take the time you need to mentally and emotionally recover; but when you're feeling defeated, ask yourself, "In what ways could I have improved?" Because if you're going to try again, you must be committed to doing better on that next attempt.

Some learning experiences will occur naturally, while others will require more conscious effort. For instance, you might naturally become more resilient with each failure, but you may need to analyze your strategies and revise your plans consciously. During my first attempt to climb Mt. Logan, I familiarized myself with the terrain. This knowledge made my second climb feel more natural and informed. That's an example of learning from failure coming naturally. Other times, you'll have to be more intentional. I waited a whole year between attempts to summit Mt. Logan, which allowed me to reflect on the unique difficulties from my first go-around. During that time, I summited two other Second Summits, and though no two mountains are the same, and the same mountain will change from one season to the next, and I would continue to run into unforeseen struggles, I still learned valuable skills. Similarly, in business, understanding the market is akin to familiarizing oneself with a mountain's terrain; timing the launch of a new company can be as crucial as choosing the right season for a climb.

Suppose you've launched a startup, and your first product release doesn't reach its projected sales. Yes, you have made some revenue, but not as much as you had hoped. There's a sense of accomplishment in bringing a product to market, but it's coupled with the reality of not meeting expectations. After that setback, it's essential to ask specific, reflective questions such as, "Did I market the product effectively?" or "Did I understand the needs of my target audience?" The objective is to learn and improve your next product launch or service offering. With enough reflection, you'll determine what you could have done better, and once the initial disappointment has subsided, pivoting your strategy is your key to being breakproof.

You might be thinking. "Jenn, that's easier said than done. Failing hurts! I put myself out there, and it didn't pan out." I get that, and I've been in your shoes. Doubt crept into the back of my mind more than I could count—a constant gnawing, like an itch you can't quite reach. That crushing pain from failure can be overwhelming, so it's vital to take the time to heal mentally and emotionally. Treat defeat like a wound; it is raw and painful and needs time to heal before you can move forward. If you'd sprained your ankle in a race, you wouldn't start training the next day, would you? That would only delay healing, and it might even make matters worse.

Take your time, be kind to yourself, and accept that setbacks are a natural part of the journey toward your goals. Then, once your sprain has healed, learn and try again. This may sound like simple, homespun advice. Good. It is.

Just Keep Climbing

On one of my expeditions, a climbing partner pointed out something I didn't know about myself: I talk to myself under my breath. At first, he wasn't sure if he was hearing things, but when he got closer, he could hear what I was saying. As I struggled to scale a cliff, strapped into a dozen pieces of equipment, and covered head to toe in layers of clothing, he could hear me whispering encouragement to myself: "Just keep climbing." My subconscious brain was looking out for me: Whenever I didn't have anyone near me to keep me going, I encouraged myself.

Cultivating persistence is key in the journey toward your goals. Setting small, achievable milestones, seeking support from friends or mentors, and regularly reflecting on your progress are all strategies that can help you maintain your resolve. Each step forward signifies success and resilience. Whenever you feel like giving up, keep climbing. You may need to become your own biggest cheerleader. I once heard Mel Robbins—author, coach, and keynote speaker—say, "If you don't believe in yourself, why should anyone else believe in you?"

Believing in yourself—and maybe even speaking to yourself in consistently positive affirmations about your ability to accomplish your goal—is part of becoming breakproof.

// REFLECTION QUESTIONS

1. Think of a setback you've faced that felt crushing at the time but later opened a new door or taught you a valuable lesson. For example, I once lost a major client that I relied heavily on, but this loss pushed me to diversify my client base, ultimately making my business more resilient. How can that experience change how you view current or upcoming moments of failure?

    _____

    _____

    _____

    _____

    _____

2. Consider a routine task, like sorting emails. How could you turn it into a game? You could set a timer and challenge yourself to organize your inbox before the time runs out and reward yourself with a short break when you succeed.

    _____

    _____

    _____

    _____

    _____

3. Are the goals you're setting achievable and inclusive for every team or family member? If not, consider breaking larger goals into smaller, tailored milestones for each member so everyone can participate and progress at their own pace. How can you ensure you all arrive together?

    _____

    _____

    _____

    _____

4. How could you be more mindful of the various sources of energy needed to fuel the pursuit of your goals (physical, emotional, mental, spiritual, etc.)? To be more mindful of your energy sources, schedule regular check-ins with yourself. Are you getting enough sleep, eating nourishing meals, taking breaks for relaxation, and engaging in activities that uplift your spirit?

    _____

    _____

    _____

    _____

5.   Who on your team are the people fighting the hardest for your success? Identify the individuals in your team who consistently support your projects and ideas. They often give constructive feedback, volunteer for tasks, and celebrate your accomplishments with you. Who are the detractors, and how can you mitigate their influence?

_____

_____

_____

_____

6.   Consider obvious risks in reaching your ambitious goals, such as financial loss or time investment. Now think broader: Have you considered the potential impact on your health, relationships, or work-life balance? How can you prepare for these less obvious risks?

_____

_____

_____

_____

7.   Reflect on a challenging experience in your personal or professional life, not as a "failure" but as a "lesson." Write down the insights you gained from that experience. How can these learnings shape your approach to future endeavors positively?

_____

_____

_____

_____

CHAPTER 3
EMBRACE THE POWER OF IMPERFECT STARTS

DYKH-TAU

Given the geopolitical tensions and visa complexities, and the war soon to be raging between Russia and Ukraine, not many people make an impromptu trip to Russia these days. Even those with the best connections and intentions find entry into the country from most of Europe and the United States nearly impossible. If it hadn't been for the right timing—fortunate alignment of political conditions—and an expert team—local friends who knew how to navigate the complex visa and permit application process—I likely wouldn't have made it to Russia to scale the second-highest peak in Europe.

Dykh-Tau,[1] located on the border of Russia and Georgia, stands at 5,055 meters (17,077 feet). The easiest path to the summit is far from easy. For the vast majority of the climb, I was actually climbing ridgelines. I teetered on rocky spines with precipitous drops on either side of me almost nonstop for three days.

As I looked up at the steep, icy ascent ahead of me, I was overwhelmed with doubt and fear, questioning whether I had the strength and skill to reach the summit. The thought of summiting under such adverse conditions seemed more like a desperate shot in the dark than

---

1   pronounced DIKH-TOW: "dikh" (rhymes with "pick") and "tau" (rhymes with "cow").

a realistic goal. From troubles making it to the country in the first place to replacing my gear (more on that later) and experiencing some of the most extreme weather phenomena I've ever encountered, the climb looked doomed from the start—hell, it was almost doomed *before* the start. I wasn't exactly in the best mental or emotional space to climb Dykh-Tau. Still reeling from my failed summit at K2 a month prior, I grappled with self-doubt, frustration, and lingering fear.

But I'm getting ahead of myself; let me take you back to the start of this adventure, where it all began with a seemingly simple decision to climb. This chapter is about imperfect starts—the unexpected and often challenging beginnings of our journeys, whether they be in mountaineering, entrepreneurship, or personal development. Embracing these imperfect starts, rather than fearing them, is a crucial step to becoming breakproof—to building the resilience we need to keep going, no matter the obstacles. Whether you're learning a new skill, launching a business or product, or starting a new workout regimen, the setbacks and speed bumps in your way sometimes make even the beginning phase more than we expect. But as Dykh-Tau taught me—and will teach you—resilience in the face of adversity can turn the imperfect starts into triumphs.

The trials of mountain climbing—like harsh weather conditions, meticulous planning, and constant problem solving—may seem worlds apart from the challenges of starting a business. But in reality, they are strikingly similar. For instance, launching a new product can feel like reaching a new altitude, where the environment is unfamiliar and the risks are high, requiring nimble adjustments, just as a climber has to adapt to changing weather conditions. Consider this: In the United States, 21 percent of new businesses fail within the first year. Just shy of 50 percent fail within five years. That means a massive percentage of all new businesses in the most entrepreneurial-favorable market in the world fail in the first five years. These statistics illustrate just how common imperfect starts are in the entrepreneurial world. Now, ask yourself why this is happening. Is it a lack of access to capital? Is it a too-short cash runway? Was there a shortage of market research? Was it a wildly changing marketplace? Was the product or service simply unremarkable? Did the owner choose to phone it in when it came to business development, marketing, and advertising?

As you're thinking about becoming breakproof, I think it's vital that you are sobered up by these statistics around entrepreneurial starts and recognize that imperfect starts are kind of the name of the game. But unless you want to **Resilience in the face** find yourself part of that new business fail rate, **of adversity can turn** you'll need to do something different. You'll need **the imperfect starts into triumph.** to embrace and understand how your imperfect start to your goal positions you for success. Only you can answer this question: Are you willing to face and embrace the rocky beginnings to persevere?

A Last-Minute Deal

Let me start with the time frame. After failing to summit K2 in August 2021, I returned home a different person. I felt like a deflated balloon, spinning from defeat; I questioned my abilities, decisions, and chosen path. It was during one of those reflective evenings back home in Park City, Utah, as I pored over maps and expedition notes, that a surprising and fateful call from Garrett Madison with Madison Mountaineering came through: "How'd you like to try for Dykh-Tau in Russia?"

I was aware of the difficulties Dykh-Tau posed. Not only was the mountain considered one of the hardest to summit (I'd probably rank it second or third most difficult of the Seven Second Summits), but getting into Russia was a herculean task in itself: the visa process was stringent, with piles of paperwork, background checks, and looming political tensions. Because of the inherent problems associated with it, I'd put Dykh-Tau on the back burner, hoping to knock out easier and more familiar summits first, having no idea that six months later, Russia would invade Ukraine and become a world pariah with the U.S. State Department forbidding all civilian travel. Talk about timing— this was right before diplomatic relations soured significantly due to

Russia's invasion of Ukraine, which I couldn't have anticipated. Had I waited, unbeknownst to me then, I may have missed the opportunity to climb Dykh-Tau. After all, that window closed potentially forever six months later. That alone would have prevented me from earning this world record.

But when fate comes knocking, you answer.

The bureaucratic gauntlet loomed before me: an obelisk of paperwork teeming with technical terms and legal jargon that required my immediate attention. And I mean immediate attention. While relations between Russia and the United States haven't been especially great for the past few decades, things were threatening to boil over in 2021 even before the Ukrainian conflict. The way I saw it, I could either be patient and wait for things to simmer down, or jump on a plane now in case things got worse. Luckily, I've always been more prone to act than wait. One of my strengths is a lifelong proclivity toward movement known to most as a jump into action or "bias to action."

I scored very high on the popular psychology assessment known as the Kolbe A Index, which measures a person's instinctive problem-solving strengths. The results indicated that I naturally respond to problems with swift, decisive action—a trait that, in this case, propelled me toward my goal. There is value associated with clearly identifying your strengths and areas of growth to ensure they're working for you instead of against you. Developing a heightened sense of self-awareness on when your strengths are overplayed and, in fact, become weaknesses also contributes to becoming breakproof. My bias to action no doubt fatigues some people around me. Still, as I look at the totality of my life, it's been essential to a disproportionate share of my success—a key to making this climb even possible. Is yours a liability or a superpower?

I spent weeks filing the permits. Each form seemed more complex than the last, and with every phone call to local authorities, I felt the weight of the language barrier and cultural differences. At night, in those quiet moments before sleep, I prayed for a miracle, for all this effort and paperwork to pay off.

It was an imperfect start, fraught with uncertainties, but it was a start—and that, I knew, was where the journey truly began.

"Are You Sure About This?"

The applications weren't the only barrier between me and Dykh-Tau. After securing my visa, I realized the road ahead was riddled with potholes. My imperfect start, marked by unexpected complications and emotional hurdles, began well before I set foot on the mountain.

After my K2 disappointment, I was initially overwhelmed by defeat. It's never easy to fall short of a goal, and this one took a greater toll on me than I liked to admit to friends and family as I arrived home, and the wound of not summitting was still fresh. Had I quit? In my heart, I knew the answer was no. Here's why I believe that. As I entered my home, naturally, the very first question my children asked me was, "So, Mom, did you summit?" And my answer was, "No, but I succeeded. I failed to summit, but I was successful because I showed up as a person I'm proud of." When faced with a decision to continue up the mountain, I elected to turn around to be there for my team and live out my value: People over peaks. When sharing this story with other adults, I added details about a fellow climbing partner and friend who died on the mountain. This belief—that "you don't get to choose how you die, but you do get to choose how you live"—has been my mantra, especially after surviving a near-death car accident in Utah. This friend, 68, single, with no immediate family, died doing what he loved, which I call dying by living. But as I navigated the emotional fog, a new opportunity emerged in the sharp, triangular form of Dykh-Tau. I filled out visa and application forms before the dust had settled. My friends and family, who saw the toll the K2 climb had taken on my physical and mental health, were justifiably worried about me. The rumors surrounding Dykh-Tau painted it as a technical monster with sheer ice walls and relentless storms. Was I ready to face another climb?

In my experience, the best antidote to failure is another attempt at success. It's the principle applied for many of us in business or when you're passed over for a promotion or when your project proposal is rejected: Try again. Likewise, in more personal goals, when you miss your target pace for that race you've been training for or you've come up short in your training, try again. In every case, picking yourself up and forging ahead is the most likely path to progress.

Still, doubt always creeps in. Were the odds in my favor for Dykh-Tau? Absolutely not. And I wasn't ignorant of that. Some of my friends were concerned that I wasn't physically able to climb again. Mountains take a lot out of you, and without adequate recovery time, you can put your long-term health at risk. Physically, I felt strong and resilient, having rigorously trained and undergone a complete medical check-up. This gave me the confidence to rebuff those concerns.

Other friends delicately broached another issue: my emotional state. They had witnessed my deep disappointment after K2 and questioned whether I had given myself enough time to heal emotionally. I might have been physically ready to face another climb,

In every case, picking yourself up and forging ahead is the most likely path to progress.

but was I emotionally prepared to face another failure? And my honest answer to them was no, I was not in a position to fail again. I was a tangle of nerves, still reeling from the haunting memories of my K2 expedition. If I didn't summit Dykh-Tau, who knows if I'd still have the drive to pursue the rest of the Seven Second Summits? And even if I did, my broken determination would be shattered even more. My friends were afraid that another failure so soon might worsen my emotional state further. These were not unreasonable concerns. My friends were my safety net, their worry was a form of care. In my journey to becoming breakproof, their voices were the cautionary tales that kept me grounded. Their opinions, insights, and assessments may not always be accurate, but they're valuable sounding boards that help me check myself. I was okay... enough. I was stable enough to consider this new challenge, but I couldn't deny the lingering ache of my previous failure.

Yet, with the emotional turmoil still churning inside me—a disconcerting mixture of fear, exhilaration, and determination to continue—the call to climb resounded just as loud as ever. I was being drawn to Dykh-Tau by an irresistible power, and who was I to reject that? The insight here is to resist suppressing your inner call to adventure. Following your instinct of pursuit, even if it ends up unsuccessful, is part of being breakproof, because success isn't always measured by accomplishing your goal; it's measured by whether or not you're expanding and growing.

If I attempted Dykh-Tau and failed, I'd be distraught. My friends and family would pick up pieces of me for months, maybe years. But to tell myself never to try? I'd be irreparably damaged. Turning my back on this challenge was out of the question. The call of the mountain echoed in my chest, growing in intensity every second, reminding me I was meant to face this challenge, no matter how daunting it might seem. I had to go. After nights of wrestling with my thoughts, I realized that I would rather face the risk than live with the regret of not trying. To put everyone's concerns to rest, I promised to prepare as best as possible. No matter the imperfect start, I'd be ready to face this mountain.

I had double-checked my gear, studied the route meticulously, engaged in mental-conditioning exercises, and even learned some basic Russian phrases to better communicate with locals. Despite all this, there was an uneasy feeling in my stomach, a whisper warning me that no amount of preparation could fully brace me for what lay ahead. I had taken every conceivable step to prepare, both physically and mentally. Yet, as I would soon discover, no amount of preparation could have readied me for the unexpected turn my journey was about to take.

A Parisian Twist of Fate

By the time September rolled around, all of my permits and visas were signed off on, and I'd assembled the perfect gear. I'd done my research, spoken with experts and fellow climbers, and put together the most effective pack I could. It was lightweight, compact, covered all my necessities, and was designed to protect me against the unexpected. I had meticulously assembled all the items I would need for this harrowing climb ahead. For those of you who engage in outdoor activities such as camping, rock climbing, or skiing, you know how crucial proper gear assembly is. It can sometimes mean the difference between life and death. My pack was done. I felt more than prepared.

But once again, the adage "expect the unexpected" proved true, a lesson I thought I'd learned by now.

At the time, there were only a handful of flights from the United States to Russia, and they all required a stop somewhere in Western Europe. In my case, I flew directly from the Salt Lake International Airport to Amsterdam, which only required a short connection to Moscow on my way to Mineralnye Vody Airport in far-flung southwest Russia. These flights connected smoothly, allowing me time to catch up on my sleep. My luck seemed primed for a successful climb ahead.

As I approached the gate to board my flight to Russia, I felt a knot tighten in my stomach. When I handed over my boarding pass, the airline staff gave me a look that told me something was wrong. "I'm sorry," she said, "but this particular flight is a repatriation flight, which means only Russians are allowed on board."

I had my visa, I had my permits, and I had my gear. And now I was being stopped halfway to my destination? Couldn't someone have told me this before I left Salt Lake City? How was I allowed to book a flight that required me to be a Russian citizen anyway? Why had this flight been an option for me in the first place?

But I couldn't quit now. Not when I was this close and success was so crucial. I talked with some very kind and informed airline employees who could sense my desperation. They told me I could catch a connecting flight to Russia at one of two different airports. Great! Now I had options.

My options? Paris or Istanbul.

So I had to find another flight and change my entire itinerary. Plus, there was the added stress of ensuring my luggage would follow me. Annoying, yes, but I considered these minor inconveniences in my epic endeavor to climb this mountain. I didn't have the time or energy to complain (no matter how badly I wanted to). I found a flight to Paris, and I was able to make the ensuing flights without a hitch.

A full day later, exhausted but relieved, I finally set foot in Russia. Only then did I receive the news that felt like a punch in the gut: my meticulously assembled gear was still in Amsterdam.

"Work With What You Have"

Somewhere between the bustling terminals of Amsterdam and the vast expanse of Russia, my luggage had been swallowed by the unforgiving logistics in the bowels of several airports. Everything I'd prepared. My goal wasn't just to climb a mountain but to set a world record; every piece of equipment in that pack was painstakingly ordered, measured, and tested as part of my process to earn this record. And it was all gone. For example, my now-missing pack contained a particular pair of gloves, chosen after trying twenty pairs back in Utah—they were essential for this technical climb. Without those gloves, not only would the climb be more dangerous, but achieving the record I was striving for was suddenly far more daunting. My gear—the one element of this journey that I felt confident about and that eased my anxiety— wouldn't join me at the mountain.

Much like in other aspects of life, I'd been thrown a curveball. It didn't matter if this mix-up happened on the side of a mountain or in a board meeting. Part of becoming breakproof is turning on a dime, using your creativity, ingenuity, resourcefulness, imagination, and resilience to find workarounds. The ability to pivot is drawn from your level of resilience. When I am faced with facts and have proved they are accurate, no matter how frustrated or incensed I may be, I practice a principle that has served me well in business and life: "Accept and move on"—an invaluable asset time and again.

The airlines told me the luggage would arrive in a couple of days, and if I waited, I could be at the airport when it arrived and on my way to the mountain the same day. My visa and permits allowed for this kind of delay, so I went to my team. There were only two guides for this climb, both native Russians: Viktor and Alekai. Viktor was a powerhouse who could carry anything and everything, and fortunately, Alekai spoke some English. Together, this combination proved to be invaluable. Other members of the team included Garrett (a tour operator) and Chase and me—the Madison Mountaineering clients. Together with Viktor, Alekai, and Garrett, our team was a total of five.

With a sinking feeling, I approached Viktor and Alekai and explained my situation. "Why don't we get a hotel and wait for my gear?" I suggested, hoping for their support. We'd have to delay the climb, but I couldn't think of any alternative. I stated my case, expecting understanding and agreement. Simply put, I was mistaken.

Part of becoming breakproof is turning on a dime, using your creativity, ingenuity, resourcefulness, imagination, and resilience to find workarounds.

"Not possible," Viktor said. "Our weather window is now."

His limited English was enough to convey a grim reality: If I wanted to climb this mountain, I would have to do so without my painstakingly selected gear, and I'd have to start now. I was incredulous.

But I wasn't without a paddle, so to speak. On the way to the mountain was a store that rented and sold all kinds of hiking and mountain climbing gear. Just about everything I needed for climbing was available for rent, although none of it in my size or—and this may seem trivial—my preferred color. Remember, climbing isn't all physical. It's also mental, and you must create small pleasures for yourself amid the sometimes harrowing challenges and tedious boredom. When I found out that the only coat close to my size was maroon, a color I've always detested, it felt like one more test of my resolve. I bought a backpack that needed a tie to pull the shoulder straps together so it wouldn't slide off my shoulders, and the boots were also way too big.

Who climbs a mountain in gear like this? Nobody… but me. We then picked up the rest of the gear I needed—meaning a toothbrush, socks, underwear, and other generic items. It's no small matter, but the socks you wear climbing one of the second-highest mountains in the world make a difference. So I bought socks. Just regular, normal socks.

Just as in life, I had to seize the options available to me, making the best of an undesirable situation. So with a thrown-together pack, random gear, and a team of guides I'd known for a full two hours, I would attempt this mountain.

The fact is only one in six teams summits. Even with perfect conditions, it's not easy. Let alone with the wrong gear, but turning back now isn't an option.

But to me, turning back would be a failure. It would mean defeat. It would mean quitting. And I was determined to see this through to the end.

"I want to do it," I said, my voice steady but my heart racing. "However far up I get, this will be a trial run. At the very least, I'll learn how to do it better next time." Just as in everyday life, every potential failure, every threat of a setback is a chance to learn, to improve, to understand better. It's not about reaching the top every time but about how we adapt, learn, and improve in every step of our journey. If nothing else, this climb, no matter how far I got, would teach me something invaluable about myself and the mountain. This experience, I realized, was its own kind of summit. It wasn't just about reaching the peak; it was about proving to myself that I could face immense challenges and keep moving forward, adapt, and survive. It was a summit of spirit and determination.

We started our ascent.

How to Avoid an Avalanche and Dodge Electricity

As I pointed out earlier, Dykh-Tau is almost entirely ridgelines all the way up, with occasional shoulder-deep snow. At times, we had to dig ourselves up the mountain. At its most basic, Dykh-Tau consists of a series of ridgelines, with a base camp at the bottom and two additional camps partway up the mountain. As you can imagine, it's no walk in the park. The dangers we faced on Dykh-Tau—avalanches and invisible electrical storms—can be likened to the challenges we face in our lives. Sometimes we have to cause some controlled chaos to prevent a bigger disaster (like starting a controlled avalanche), and other times we have to constantly stay alert to the forces around us, respect them, and bide our time before we move forward again (like in an electrical storm). Both situations—whether navigating avalanches and electrical storms on a mountain or facing life's unexpected challenges—require awareness, courage, and wisdom. Just as we strategically navigated Dykh-Tau's risks, in life we must also assess our situations, make calculated decisions, and sometimes wait patiently for the right moment to act.

For Dykh-Tau, our climbing included trudging through chest-high snow and straddling ridges with specialized gear and crampons.

Just to lay on another heap of danger, Dykh-Tau is avalanche-prone. In the Caucasus Mountains, Dykh-Tau is directly between the Black Sea and the Caspian Sea. With all that moisture and wind, the snow that falls is loose and prone to break off in large chunks along the mangled ridgelines, resulting in frequent avalanches.

However, my guides showed me how to avoid avalanches: Start one under controlled conditions. Though it may seem counterintuitive, creating smaller, controlled avalanches can reduce the risk of a larger one that will catch you unawares. Sometimes when they tried to trigger an avalanche, it would happen, and sometimes it wouldn't. Regardless of the outcome, we could move forward with greater confidence. It's reminiscent of businesses that hire experts to test the vulnerabilities of their software systems; you hope they can't penetrate the defenses, but if they do, you're relieved it's your trusted professional and not a malicious intruder. But these avalanche triggers were only attempted by experienced professionals under very specific conditions. Let me

repeat: *Don't start an avalanche unless you know what you're doing.*
It takes years of experience and training and can still pose serious
risks. I never started an avalanche myself because of the danger, even
though I'd climbed more than my fair share of snow-ridge mountains
in my time.

Viktor and Alekai knew what they were doing. Now and then, one
would stay with me, and the other climbers would continue on the
path for a few hundred feet. Carefully and very
hesitantly, they would walk along the very top of   **Some of the most**
the ridgeline, disturbing the snow at the very top   **dangerous storms**
in a line, hoping for things to loosen up. A few   **are invisible.**
minutes later, a wall of snow would go careening down the
mountainside, and we'd get the all-clear to keep moving forward. It
was a precarious but proven solution to a deadly problem.

The weather had more than one ace up its sleeve, however. On the
third and final day, about an hour from the summit, Viktor told me a
storm was coming. With decades of experience, he could sense danger
in subtle changes in the air, a skill that had saved many lives. We had
to turn around. I was floored, not only because he told me we were
going to give up but because the weather was mild at worst. We were
up in the clouds, so it was foggy, but other than that, we were fine.
How could this be a storm? I urged us to press forward. And when I say
urged, I mean pleaded. I was summiting this mountain. He acquiesced,
and we continued our ascent.

What I learned was that some of the most dangerous storms are
invisible. There's an uncommon weather phenomenon that sometimes
takes place in the Caucasus Mountains range called electrical storms.
"Uh, Jenn?" you might be thinking, "I know what a thunderstorm
is. They happen everywhere." I didn't say thunderstorm. I said
electrical storm.

We got to the summit of Dykh-Tau, and after two quick photos, as
we headed down, the weather had a weird energy; we needed to get
off the mountain. All of a sudden, I thought to myself, "Weird. Why

is my back hot?" I hadn't been anything near warm in days. Now it felt like I was on fire. It turns out, when you're in the clouds and they have an electrical charge in them (like during a thunderstorm), they'll attach to anything that can hold that charge, and suddenly your metal objects start heating up like they're in a convection oven.

"Hit the ground!" Viktor yelled. The only way to avoid getting electrocuted or cooked alive in these electrical storms is to ground your gear (and yourself). Once we felt the electrical current die down, we continued walking. Then it felt like I was getting pelted by hail, even though I couldn't see any. The electricity started bouncing off my forehead in small, consistent jolts. Back on the ground! It was as if we were inside a live electrical circuit, the charge seeking a path through our bodies and gear.

This situation, which I hadn't encountered before and still baffles me to this day, felt eerily similar to facing unexpected setbacks in life. Just as the storm forced me to pause and respect the forces around me, life's challenges often require us to step back, reassess, and approach our problems with caution and humility. The kinds of hurdles in our way are often unexpected and incomprehensible. You try to wrap your mind around them and become more confused. Sometimes the only way forward is to hit the ground and wait for the turmoil to pass. It's not about cowering in fear but about wisely understanding the stakes of the situation and acting accordingly.

After two hours of dodging electricity, army crawling, and slithering down the mountain, our bodies pressed against the icy, unforgiving earth as electricity sparked and popped like it was cackling in the air above us, we'd finally made it down to a point low enough on the mountain where the electricity was less of a threat. Despite every hurdle—my second-string gear, a limited shared vocabulary, and permits with ink that had barely dried—I persevered. In a moment that made every challenge worth the expense, I found myself safely back at camp. Many celebrate summits, but that is only the halfway point; returning to camp that night, finally out of danger, was the true success. The start may have been far from perfect, and I may have literally crawled to the finish line, but I'd succeeded.

Just as I didn't let an imperfect start deter me from seeing my goal through to the end, life will throw curveballs your way time and time again. But the start doesn't define the journey. It's one step in the process, and one that can be recovered from in the event of less-than-ideal beginnings. Your destination is still in front of you, so climb your **The start doesn't define the journey.** mountain, scale your ridgeline, and brave your slopes. Like the climb, life doesn't promise clear paths. Whether a vertical ice wall or a personal tragedy, each challenge demands that we assess, learn, and adapt. It is not the absence of obstacles but how we navigate them that defines our journey.

In the end, despite countless obstacles and overwhelming odds, my journey up Dykh-Tau became a vivid metaphor for life. Even when faced with a hazardous beginning, I persevered and achieved what seemed impossible. It taught me that no matter how steep our mountains appear, with determination and resilience, we can reach our summits.

BE BREAKPROOF: HOW TO EMBRACE THE POWER OF IMPERFECT STARTS

1. **Be Prepared Despite Uncertainties.** Preparation is key for any endeavor. For example, before my climb up Dykh-Tau, I consulted with experienced climbers and studied the weather patterns, despite knowing the inherent unpredictability of mountain weather. This research proved invaluable when we encountered unexpected storms. Gathering the right tools and continually adapting, even when plans fall apart, is crucial to being breakproof.

2. **Prepare Emotionally.** Whether it's scaling mountains or starting a new business, the path will not always be smooth. It's essential to assess if you're emotionally ready for a new challenge, especially after a failure. Consider practices like meditation, counseling, or journaling to process emotions, and build a support network of trusted friends or mentors to help assess your emotional state.

3. **Expect the Unexpected.** Even with thorough planning, unforeseen challenges may arise. It's essential to remain flexible and adaptable, able to adjust your plans as needed. Just because the beginning of your journey doesn't go as planned doesn't mean you can't reach your goal. Continue to push forward, and don't let an imperfect start discourage you.

4. **Take Timely Action.** Sometimes you must take a calculated risk and seize the opportunity when it presents itself. A bias toward action, despite perceived liabilities, can often be the difference between success and failure.

5. **Use Your Resources and Creativity.** When faced with difficulties, employ your ingenuity, resourcefulness, creativity, and imagination to find workarounds. For instance, when my gear failed on Dykh-Tau, I improvised with materials I had, reinforcing my equipment with duct tape and carabiners. Seize available options: Even when the situation seems undesirable, make the best of the options available to you.

6. **Understand Your Strengths and Weaknesses.** Knowing your strengths can guide you to success, while understanding your weaknesses helps mitigate potential risks. For example, my determination led me to attempt the summit of Dykh-Tau, while recognizing my inexperience with electrical storms helped me heed my guide's warnings.

7. **Follow Your Inner Call to Adventure.** Even if the chances of success are slim, trusting your instinct can lead to personal growth and resilience. For instance, despite the slim odds, I followed my passion for climbing and embarked on a challenging journey that shaped my character far beyond reaching any summit. Success is often measured by personal growth and expansion rather than just achieving the initial goal.

8. **Respect the Forces Around You.** Understand the potential dangers or challenges and prepare for them. This could be the possibility of avalanches during a mountain climb or the risks involved in a business venture. Awareness, courage, and wisdom are essential.

9. **Leverage Failure to Drive Success.** Failure should not be a roadblock but a stepping stone to success. After my unsuccessful attempt at climbing K2, I analyzed what went wrong and used those lessons to prepare more effectively for my Dykh-Tau expedition. Every setback or potential failure is a chance to learn, improve, and understand better. It's not just about reaching the top but about how we adapt, learn, and improve in every step of our journey.

10. **Accept and Move On.** Don't dwell on setbacks. Instead, accept them and keep moving forward. After a storm threatened to turn us back just an hour from the summit, it was potentially devastating; but I had to accept that safety came first. Facing difficulties head-on and persevering, even in the face of failure, can lead to eventual triumphs. Remember, the journey itself is often the most significant achievement.

UTILIZING YOUR IMPERFECT START

You may be waiting for the right moment to begin chasing your goals. Whether it's when you have more free time, a little more cash on hand, or more experience, you may be stalling before putting the pedal to the metal.

While there's something to say about timing, there's just as much to say about taking a stab at your goals when things aren't perfect. There's no real *perfect* start—any beginning will have its imperfections. The sooner you figure out how to correct and even embrace an imperfect start, the sooner you'll be on your way to achieving your goals. And as always, rolling with the punches from an imperfect start is how you become more resilient and breakproof.

Name the Imperfections

When dealing with an imperfect start, your first step toward your destination is taking account of the imperfections at play. Not all imperfections are created equal. A lack of free time differs vastly from a lack of funds or resources, which is also different from poor timing or unfortunate mistakes.

When I decided to climb Dykh-Tau, there were many reasons why I shouldn't try. When talking with very close friends and family members, many perceived reservations were shared with me, most based on their fears, not mine. But I am grateful to those who helped me outline the real issues! Because when you can name the imperfections, you can understand them, and the more you understand them, the better you are at solving the problem. Take a moment to list your own perceived imperfections or obstacles. Are they based on your own assessment, or influenced by others' opinions?

> The sooner you figure out how to correct and even embrace an imperfect start, the sooner you'll be on your way to achieving your goals.

While my experience involved mountaineering, the process of identifying and overcoming imperfections is applicable in any context.

Let's take a look at some of the problems that contributed to my imperfect start on Dykh-Tau:

- **I didn't have the right gear.** Mountaineering is different from other athletic endeavors because the "field" or "court" is never the same. Even when climbing the same mountain twice, weather conditions and changes in terrain from one year to the next will shift how you approach it. Preparing the right gear for each climb is of the utmost importance. With limited time to prepare for Dykh-Tau, I lacked the necessary gear.

- **I wasn't in a good headspace.** Any athlete will tell you that your mental game is just as important (if not more important) than your physical prowess. Mountaineering is no different. Any mountain you climb will try to break your spirit and crush your hopes. Coming off of my first failed summit, I wasn't in a very good emotional and mental frame to blindly take another stab at a mountain that was just as difficult as the last one.

- **Getting to Russia was complicated.** I'd known about this before my impromptu attempt. Russia doesn't welcome many Americans into their country with open arms. From visas to permits, I'd need help and a little luck if I wanted to get close to the mountain's base, let alone the summit.

So having identified these major imperfections, how did acknowledging them enable me to confront, adapt, and embrace this imperfect start?

- **I didn't have the right gear,** *so I dove into research and previous experience*. Working with people who had attempted Dykh-Tau before and finding as much help as I could online and through my networks, I learned which pieces of equipment were absolutely necessary, which were nice to have, and which I could leave behind. I knew not only what I needed to bring but also *why* I needed to bring it. This preparation helped me pivot when I lost my gear before landing in Russia. (In case you were wondering, my luggage made it to Russia right before I flew home. Lucky me... I guess.)

- **I wasn't in a good headspace,** *but adjusting the goal was the antidote.* Everyone is different when it comes to mental health. When dealing with disappointment and defeat, your necessities for healing will differ widely from what may help me or your team member or whoever else is in a rut. I knew that if I used my failed summit as a reason to take a break, I would be far less likely to meet my goal than if I jumped right back in the saddle. Furthermore, I adjusted what success would look like for this climb, leaning away from summiting and toward collecting data and gaining experience. For that reason, attempting Dykh-Tau improved my mental health, even if it came with a risk of failing to summit again. In your journey, consider whether adjusting your goals, rather than abandoning them, could be a valuable approach when facing mental or emotional setbacks.

- **Getting to Russia was complicated,** *so I had to get started now.* A good deal of my success in getting to Russia comes down to luck and having good connections in the mountaineering community. I learned expert ways to expedite the process, such as reaching out to experienced climbers for advice on faster visa applications and engaging a local guide who could assist with permits, all of which required immediate action. Remember: bias to action. Keep in mind that this was the kind of issue that would guarantee *any* start would be an imperfect start. There was no avoiding this one: I just had to do it. Faced with a complicated process to enter Russia, I recognized the need for immediate and decisive action. In your endeavors, don't let complex procedures deter you. Start early and seek advice from those with experience.

Solutions often appear once you've identified the imperfections in your start. It's not the absence of imperfections that defines your journey, but your ability to navigate them that leads to growth. So, what imperfect start will you embrace today?

Gather Your Tools, Prepare Your Team

Continuing on the foundation laid in the last chapter about "building based on strengths," you must remember that the key is to start with what you have and use it as your building blocks.

An imperfect start is normal; often it comes with some warning sign, or at the very least, a small cushion of time before the rubber meets the road. What can you do in the meantime? Get ready! No, you don't have all the time in the world. Yes, it would be great if you could catch a breather. But you don't, and you can't. These are the cards you were dealt, and now all you have left to do is play your hand. In any situation, whether it's learning a violin concerto under a tight deadline or launching a project with limited resources, the steps remain similar: Inform your support network, assess what you can realistically accomplish, and tailor your approach accordingly.

What do you do? Gather your tools and prepare your team. Tools in this context refer to the resources and strategies you can employ, such as new techniques, mentor advice, or reference materials. Your "team" here doesn't necessarily mean a formal group; it refers to your support networks, such as mentors, teachers, friends, family, or even online communities who can guide and encourage you. By acting decisively and using the resources at your disposal, you set yourself on a course for progress, no matter how challenging the initial steps may be.

Imperfect Middles

While we've previously discussed the challenges of imperfect starts, it's equally important to consider what happens when you run into an issue halfway through your journey—what I call the "imperfect middles." You've already put so much time, effort, and energy into this goal, then suddenly the rug is pulled out from under you. At this point, you might ask, "Why even try?" Feeling frustrated and demotivated is natural when your hard work seems to unravel.

This is where imperfect starts might help you rather than hurt you. One of the excellent skills you learn from working with imperfect starts is how to improvise. You learn to discern which aspects of the process are vital—like maintaining your vision and adapting your plan—and what can be discarded—like a rigid timeline or peripheral tasks. You'll quickly realize how much of your checklist is there for comfort and convenience rather than survival.

When you're struck with an imperfect middle, two methods will help get you through: Burn bridges and create small milestones.

For me, my imperfect middle was twofold: being told I couldn't board my flight and losing my luggage. In both cases, my experiences making it that far had prepared me to pivot and adapt, finding a different flight and renting gear in Russia that worked well enough to get me to the summit. To pivot, I had to metaphorically "burn a bridge" behind me—meaning that I had to mentally close off the option of returning home and focus on finding a new path forward. I chose a different flight via Paris to Russia rather than a flight home because a return home would have meant quitting. I had to mentally eliminate an option that would lead me to square one, which left me with only options that led me closer to my goal.

One of the excellent skills you learn from working with imperfect starts is how to improvise.

Burning bridges, in this context, doesn't mean severing relationships or acting rashly. It means deliberately choosing to leave certain options behind, making it easier to focus on constructive paths forward. Burning bridges behind you works in messy middles because it only leaves you with forward-moving choices. One of the significant differences between messy beginnings and messy middles is how close you feel to safety. In a messy beginning, you feel like you can turn around easily. You're just outside your front step, and you haven't invested a lot into the success of your goal, so the cost to turn back isn't high. When you're stuck in the middle, however, the path home and the path to your goal seem equally fraught with danger. You feel helpless. In these chaotic spaces, it becomes easy for overwhelming thoughts and emotions to suffocate you. By cutting out half of your options (turning back), you can ease that burden slightly. Yes, you're still uncertain, but you know which direction you're heading.

Let's imagine you're starting your own business. You may have entered the scene when the economy wasn't doing great, but you'd survived thus far. Then you get hit with supply-chain issues. It may feel like the universe is conspiring against you, but you can always fight back. What lessons did you learn from entering an unfavorable economy, and how can you burn a bridge so forward is the only choice left? You may have had to take on extra responsibilities and make quick connections with others in your industry. What are they doing now? Is their bottom line being hit like yours? Do they have other suppliers that you can rely on too? Maybe they're keeping their cards close to their chest. No matter. How did you find your current supplier in the first place? Can you use the same tools and navigate the same avenues to find another supplier? These questions aren't just about solving an immediate problem—they're a way of mentally "burning bridges," leaving behind the option to quit and focusing instead on finding solutions. All of them are pointed toward continuing your business. Not one of them is directed toward folding, declaring bankruptcy, or worrying about getting eaten up by the competition. That is how you "burn bridges" effectively: by asking questions that guide you toward solutions and progress rather than toward giving up.

The second key to navigating the messy middle is creating small milestones. Amid the chaos, breaking down your journey into more minor, more manageable steps can bring clarity and focus, essentially shortening your miles. Let me take you back to my own experience for a moment. When I hit the messy middle of Dykh-Tau, I had to change what success and progress looked like. Because the mountain is one ridgeline after another, the most natural way to measure progress is one ridgeline at a time. However, when morale was low, and even one step forward felt like a monumental struggle, I shortened my milestones. I didn't measure progress by ridgelines but by the few yards before me. And by changing my mindset, I changed how I perceived success, giving myself that little extra kick of serotonin that kept me engaged through the messy middle.

Just as those shortened milestones were essential for me on Dykh-Tau, they can be a lifeline for you in the thick of difficult times. When you're feeling just as far from where you want to go as where you started, shortening the distance between milestones will help keep you engaged. You might be tempted to think you're patting yourself on the back too much, but it's not self-indulgence—it's a survival strategy. Celebrating these small wins is giving yourself the momentum needed to continue.

An imperfect middle may be messy, but it's not a dead end. With the right mindset and strategies, you're not just surviving but paving your path to triumph.

Embracing the Philosophy of "At the Very Least"

I was exhausted before I even made it to base camp at Dykh-Tau. Imperfect starts have a way of sapping the energy out of you before you even begin. In that drained state, I found solace in a simple yet powerful mindset: the philosophy of "at the very least."

When chasing a goal, it's easy to believe that anything less than 100 percent success equates to failure. The problem with this mindset is that it undermines and devalues any progress you make unless you achieve the goal in its entirety. If you start your venture with the idea that you'll glean insights, even if not everything pans out as planned, setbacks won't derail you completely. For instance, if you set out to launch a startup and only secure a few clients or customers in the first months, "at the very least," you've begun to understand the market dynamics and have some early feedback to refine your approach.

Failure will still sting; it's natural to feel disappointment when we fall short. But adopting the "at the very least" philosophy can transform that disappointment into a source of motivation and learning. With this perspective, that failure becomes a teacher rather than a cruel end, guiding us toward future success. When you view it as a means of gaining valuable insight and experience along with reaching your goal, you've already fought half the battle. Plus, you give yourself the momentum to fight the other half. Not only will you get the information you're hoping for, but you'll be more eager to try harder things. After all, "at the very least," you've done better than before.

Let's consider another practical example to illustrate further how this philosophy works. Imagine you're launching a new business product and didn't get as much market research as you wanted; you may be tempted to delay or cancel the launch. However, *at the very least*, you'll likely get feedback from real users. *At the very least*, you'll understand which features or aspects of your product resonate or need improvement. *At the very least*, you'll learn valuable insights about market reception and positioning. And all of those "at the very leasts" are valuable for your ultimate journey of becoming breakproof—that is, developing the tenacity to keep pushing forward despite setbacks.

Embracing this "at the very least" attitude builds resilience and creates a space for pleasant surprises. Who knows? You might even exceed your own expectations and achieve your goal anyway. My summit of Dykh-Tau serves as a testament to this. It wasn't a journey without obstacles. Far from it. There were numerous setbacks, but I used the "at the very least" philosophy—celebrating each small progress, each lesson learned—which kept me moving upward, step by step. If it can turn my seemingly insurmountable challenges into surmountable steps, imagine what adopting the "at the very least" philosophy could do for your journey toward your goals.

// REFLECTION QUESTIONS

1.   Many people wait for the perfect conditions before taking the first step toward their dreams. Are you one of them? If so, what could you do right now to start progressing toward your goal, despite your "imperfect" environment?

_____

_____

_____

_____

_____

_____

2.   In the context of risk management, think of a "controlled avalanche" as a small, manageable step that prevents a larger, unmanageable situation. What such action could you initiate now to reduce future risks? For example, could you buy a month's pass to the gym before committing to a year, thereby discovering if you enjoy it enough to attend regularly?

_____

_____

_____

_____

_____

_____

_____

3.   What tools can you gather to help you achieve your goal? These could include educational courses for training, specialized software for managing tasks, hardware like a new computer, equipment for a home gym, or hiring a coach for personalized guidance.

_____

_____

_____

_____

_____

_____

_____

4.   Recall earlier discussions about the dangers of an "all or nothing" mentality. Why do you think this mentality can be a significant barrier to becoming breakproof? Reflect on your own experiences: Were there instances where failing to reach 100 percent of a goal still allowed you to make meaningful progress or taught you an important lesson?

_____

_____

_____

_____

_____

CHAPTER 4
SET YOURSELF UP FOR SUPPORT

MT. KENYA

Before I take you on the journey to Mt. Kenya, I want to highlight a fundamental lesson this climb reinforced: the necessity of a strong support system in becoming breakproof. We are, by nature, interdependent beings. This interdependence becomes apparent at various stages of our lives—when we are utterly reliant on others as infants or in our later years, and when we strive for independence, as I observe daily with the teenagers in my bustling and often chaotic home.

In truth, regardless of our age or life stage, we need support systems. These systems scale up during our struggles and scale down when life is smooth sailing, but they are always essential. They encompass our families, friends, colleagues, neighbors, community members, mentors, and allies. Your unique journey will likely shape the support system you cultivate.

My climbing expeditions have vividly illustrated this for me. On one notable ascent, entire school systems tracked my progress daily via GPS. Social platforms buzzed with updates about my climb—often before I was aware. Messages of encouragement flooded in from around the world, from close friends and strangers. Initially, I'd been reluctant to publicize my journey via social media. Still, after listening to an overwhelming number of friends insist on it, I agreed to open up and share updates and posts along the way. After all, should I succeed, I'd be making history.

Yet, support isn't always cloaked in praise. During these climbs, I encountered my share of critics—those quick to question my motivations, parenting, and character with little more than a cursory glance at my life. It was a hard lesson to learn, but eventually, I came to see even this criticism as a form of support. Instead of letting the negativity weigh me down, I chose to view it as a challenge—a push to prove myself and refine my approach. It became fuel, not a deterrent, transforming negative energy into a driving force propelling me toward my goals. In a sense, I learned to see criticism as an unintended compliment, often revealing more about the critic's insecurities than about my journey.

This lesson became all the more poignant during my Mt. Kenya expedition. My planned climbing team, a crucial part of my support system, was grounded by a new COVID outbreak, unable to leave the United States. This was a devastating blow, and I felt a wave of isolation and uncertainty. This unexpected hurdle demanded that I lean on a wider, albeit more remote, network of supporters—including local guides, the international climbing community, and my family back home—all of whom were with me in spirit, if not in person.

I share this at the outset to underline the transformative power of community and support systems. As you read on and perhaps reflect on your own "mountains," I hope you are inspired to cultivate a robust support system tailored to your unique path and challenges.

The second on my list, Mt. Kenya is located (you guessed it) in Kenya and stands at 5,199 meters (17,057 feet) at the summit. As I packed my gear, carefully selecting the ropes and harnesses needed for the intricate rock faces of Mt. Kenya, I couldn't help but grapple with a sense of doubt. Was I genuinely ready, both mentally and physically, for what lay ahead? And was I climbing for the right reasons or merely chasing another "high"? These questions whirled through my mind, further intensifying the weight of the upcoming journey.

In hindsight, it was strange to me how much resistance I felt within myself at the onset of this journey. Was it fear or perhaps a waning passion for my goal? I was confused. For one, I had wanted to save Mt. Kenya for later, since it required a degree of rock-climbing ability I wasn't confident in just yet. The technical routes of Mt. Kenya, including the famed Nelion and Batian peaks, were daunting. However, when a friend asked me for help with a charitable endeavor and Kenya announced that it was loosening COVID-19 regulations, I took advantage of the opportunity. Still, even with the stars aligning, I had to goad myself to get up and start the process. Without my friend's insistence, I'm not sure how earnestly I would have tried to reach my goal in the first place. The truth is, as excited as I was about the climb, a part of me was hesitant. Why? After conquering previous peaks, I surprisingly felt underwhelmed—a reaction I hadn't expected, given the magnitude of the accomplishment. This unexpected emotional flatness made me question my eagerness for this next expedition.

A Threefold Journey

I had just finished Ojos del Salado, the first of the Seven Second Summits, which was meant to be one of the most accessible mountains on the list. Coming home from that experience, however, I was feeling... meh. I'd checked Ojos del Salado off my list, but I wasn't exactly thrilled by it. The monotonous climb, with its seemingly endless stretches of barren, rocky terrain, left more than a little to be desired, and I began wondering if my goal would even be fun to accomplish. Yes, I know not everything worthwhile will give me a rush or butterflies in my stomach, but I at least wanted to have a good time.

Because of my experience with Ojos del Salado, my enthusiasm for the next mountain was notably dampened. Maybe once things slowed down and I had more time, I'd get back to scaling the Seven Second Summits. Besides, as far as I knew, nobody else was racing me for the title of first woman to complete all seven peaks. Why rush?

Just when I was questioning my next steps, my phone rang. My friend Kate's call would end up changing my perspective entirely. This conversation helped me realize that sometimes motivation doesn't always have to come from intrinsic sources or be about personal growth. Sometimes helping others can be a springboard for our personal development.

"Do you think you could do me a favor?" Kate asked.

"Sure, what is it?"

"I'm working with this charity that's delivering an ambulance to a needy community in Kenya. That's where one of your mountains is, right? Do you think you can deliver the ambulance on your way?"

Yes, Mt. Kenya was on the list of Seven Second Summits, which I'd shared with Kate before my first climb. But climbing another mountain wasn't anywhere near the top of my priority list at that time. My focus was on parenting my seven children and running my thriving yet demanding financial-services business.

However, the opportunity to help a friend and a community in need pulled at my heartstrings.

When I researched the local culture and challenges, I learned that girls in Kenya struggle with access to feminine hygiene products; this affects their ability to attend school regularly, and the situation materially stunts their academic success and, thus, their education. I knew I had to do something. So on top of delivering Kate's ambulance (not literally, but my job was to act as an ambassador for this service organization to ensure its delivery), I agreed to work with another charity to deliver feminine pads to Nairobi.

Your journey might ripple beyond your achievement.

Looking back, I never expected that one of the unintended impacts of achieving this world record would be helping young women access improved healthcare related to their menstrual cycles. But that's precisely what happened. I was privileged to provide more than four hundred women with enough sanitary products to ensure they would not miss a school day for an entire year. I share this to emphasize the profound, unexpected ways your journey might ripple beyond your achievement. I am deeply grateful to have played a role in this. It was a poignant reminder of the everyday comforts that I, and many others, often take for granted.

This request from Kate transformed my perspective. Now, with an opportunity to make a tangible difference for others, I set out for Kenya with a renewed sense of purpose. Much like in life, when we contribute to the betterment of others, it brings a sense of fulfillment that is deeply rewarding and often helps push us forward in pursuing our goals. With bags packed not just with climbing gear but also with boxes of sanitary products destined for Kenyan schools, I was more than ready to do what I could to help those in need. And there it was— my dual mission. Not only would I be climbing a formidable mountain, but I would also be embarking on a journey to deliver much-needed aid. This mission, it turned out, was the missing piece that turned my "meh" into a profound sense of purpose and excitement for the climbs ahead.

Challenges of Advocacy and Understanding

Landing in Nairobi, Kenya, I was surrounded by a vibrant, colorful landscape and a bustling community and culture. I felt an overwhelming gratitude for the opportunity to travel to this amazing country. Each day, I encountered remarkable people who helped me in my journey as I came to help them in theirs. As I dropped off each humanitarian delivery, I got closer to Mt. Kenya. Soon enough, I found myself standing at the base of the mountain, what I hoped would be my second successful climb on my Second Summits list. As it would turn out, the mountain wasn't the only obstacle I was trying to overcome.

In the United States, we shout "Down with the patriarchy!" as much as possible. And I've done my fair share of yelling—the fight for women's rights has been ongoing for over a century. The patriarchy represents oppressive attitudes and systems that have tried to frame women as secondary citizens and unequal participants in the various aspects of everyday life. And while I agree we still have a long way to go in the fight for equal rights, the issues in the United States aren't nearly as pronounced as in other countries. In some ways, this journey to Kenya was a stark wake-up call for me. At home, where I might be subtly discredited or questioned regarding my expertise because I'm a woman, the attitude toward me in Kenya was much more thinly veiled. Actually, there was almost no veil.

In addition to my guide, my climbing expedition up Mt. Kenya comprised twenty local men—not as a posse, but as essential members of the expedition team—hired to assist with various tasks, from carrying equipment to providing local knowledge of the terrain. Their employment was not a luxury for me but a complex human endeavor, a conscious effort to provide income in a difficult time; the economic hardship brought on by the COVID crisis worldwide was palpable, especially in Africa, so these gentlemen had no sources of income. These twenty people were not helping me climb the mountain; they were helping to lighten my load. I hired them for purposes as trivial as carrying my boots. Yes. One man was carrying my boots—that's it. Did I need him to? Absolutely not. Did he need the money I gave him to have him take my boots? Absolutely. In this way, my expedition became more than a climb—it became a small, temporary economy. Another example of how your own "expedition" can impact people in inconceivable and unintended ways. I share this to highlight a silver lining during a challenging time—an opportunity to support local individuals and families through employment.

Furthermore, beyond financial support, I actively sought to foster a respectful and equitable relationship with my team. I prioritized learning from them about their experiences and culture, and we shared our stories and skills. I hoped to make the expedition a true partnership. This was my way of acknowledging the complex dynamics and striving to approach our interactions with sensitivity and respect. Unfortunately, the gender divide in mountaineering is pervasive, originating from years of unequal treatment of men and women in America and globally. Although strides have been made, there still needs to be more women climbers, guides, and porters in the mountaineering community worldwide. In other mountaineering expeditions, I was given much more leeway to have my voice heard for consideration. Unless it was a concern for my safety during a perilous pass, I could take the mountain at my own pace and take my place anywhere in the line of climbers. In Kenya, what was a new experience for me was how openly my guides resisted some of my suggestions and expertise.

Even if my expertise was sometimes questioned, however, on all fronts, I felt encouraged in my journey. While some older generations still held on to the stereotypes, my experiences with Kenyans my age and younger exhibited an overwhelming hopefulness for equality.

But my journey was about more than my struggle with overt sexism. As I navigated these external challenges, I also had to confront the deeper layers of power at play. I was a white woman from America climbing a mountain in Africa, and I

When we come to the table hungry, we make very different choices than when we have full bellies.

was acutely aware of the dynamics this situation created. Recognizing my privilege, I aimed to approach my interactions with humility and respect. I listened more than I spoke, sought to learn from the local culture, and constantly evaluated how my actions might be perceived. My privileged position, while allowing me to help, risked reinforcing the narrative of a "white savior." This complex dynamic of help and hierarchy was not lost on me, and it was a challenge to strike a balance between providing assistance without usurping or disrespecting local culture and self-efficacy. Resisting the local culture, customs, and expectations, if not approached with understanding, care, and attention, could only worsen matters for everyone. It was a unique scenario I had to keep top of mind. When we come to the table hungry, we make very different choices than when we have full bellies. Therefore, the battles I chose to fight held significant weight. I had to approach the terrain with respect at the forefront and assert my rights as second in command. Each decision came with its share of introspection and a measured understanding of the intricate social dynamics. I stood up for myself when my humanity was being questioned, but I respected local customs in all ways possible. While my determination might have surprised some local guides, I was committed to demonstrate that women can excel in challenging environments just as men can. Throughout this, I aimed to maintain respect for local expertise and cultural norms.

It was a complex situation I faced, but one I had to navigate appropriately. Kenya has a rich history and vibrant culture, which I had to acknowledge and adjust to as a foreigner. Standing up for myself and advocating for equal rights couldn't come at the cost of disrespecting their culture or values, especially having not grown up or spent a significant amount of time there. It was a constant balancing act—negotiating my role as a woman in a traditionally male-dominated field while also being a respectful and conscious visitor in a foreign country. In many ways, I was navigating the figurative mountains of cultural expectations, gender roles, and privilege. Understanding this, I took the time to educate myself about the Kenyan culture and customs, actively engaging with my guides and team to foster more profound mutual respect.

But the challenges I faced weren't solely cultural or societal. In addition to these metaphorical mountains, I still had a literal mountain ahead of me. With its steep crags and jagged ridgelines, sheer cliffs, stark escarpments, and rugged precipices, the mountain stood raw and unforgiving. Mt. Kenya, in particular, offered scant places of respite; it was treacherous nearly 95 percent of the time. Just the month before, three climbers had tragically lost their lives attempting its peaks—a startling number given the relatively few who dare its ascent. Furthermore, climbing at the equator added a race against time, as daylight there lasts only 12 hours, shutting off almost like a light switch. Navigating such a dangerous mountain in the dark with only a headlamp is far from ideal. I was rock climbing to a summit for the first time, and unlike other mountains, the opportunities to regain focus, breathe deeply, and appreciate the scenery were rare. Nonetheless, these breaks were invaluable moments for personal reflection and reconnection with my deeper motivations.

I was missing my children—five boys and two girls—particularly my twin daughters, ten years old at the time of this writing. My daughters and I naturally have a special bond, and I carried a photograph of all my children tucked securely in my jacket pocket, a tangible reminder of why I pushed forward. I was showing these two powerful young girls that they can achieve anything and everything they desire if they are willing to become breakproof. They will fail. They will stop. They will pause. They will recalibrate. They will experience fears and setbacks just like they will experience successes and triumphs. In my quest to become the first woman to complete the Seven Second Summits, I was proving to my daughters that I could proudly be a woman in a male-dominated field. They were learning that they, too, could face immense challenges and conquer them in whatever path they choose.

As I contemplated Kenya's complex social dynamics, the physical journey continued unabated. Days of hiking and acclimating came and went, with our team braving the elements and scaling cliff faces. With every step, the air grew thinner, the terrain rougher. Conversely, the views were more majestic until we reached Nelion, the pinnacle nearest the summit of Mt. Kenya—the second highest point of this imposing African wonder. However, we still had a maze of ridges between us and the summit. The biting cold nipped at our exposed skin, and the gusty winds threatened to knock us off balance. And it was veiled in fog. Each step felt like a leap of faith, trusting in our training and instincts as visibility was reduced to mere feet in front of us. As I carefully placed my foot on the icy path, my goal became clearer in that fog: to summit and inspire my daughters.

The Gates of Mist

Nelion is only 11 meters (33 feet) lower than the actual highest summit of Mt. Kenya, known as Batian. Surprisingly, many mountaineers declare victory at Nelion, but as you would expect, not *this* mountaineer. Why? Because I was becoming breakproof, developing the resilience and determination to pursue my goals, no matter the obstacles. There is a six-hour climb between the two peaks, a grueling path marked by steep ridges, precarious ledges, and the ever-present, bone-chilling mist. All the moisture in the area collects between the two peaks, so I had to walk in an almost constant fog. This is where the area gets its name: the Gates of Mist. Similarly, life often presents us with stretches of uncertainty, where the path ahead is obscured, and progress seems unmeasurably small. However, in these moments, we must push forward with trust in our preparation, support system, and determination to see our goals through.

Once we got to Nelion, a disagreement arose with the guide. "We're at the top," he kept saying. "We're at the top. Nelion is the top."

"No, it's not," I said.

A key lesson in this summit is that some people declare victory early. Sometimes it's cheating. Sometimes it's cutting corners. Sometimes it's spinning or manipulating. Sometimes it's just lying. On your journey to becoming breakproof, it's vital that you be true to yourself about what accomplishment looks like. I realized that it's perfectly valid to recalibrate your goals along this journey based on new insights or conditions. And if things don't work out the first time, stopping and trying again isn't a sign of defeat—it's a new beginning. But never declare victory against a goal you didn't accomplish. Be honest with yourself because, ultimately, if you're accountable to anyone, it is to yourself.

We must push forward with trust in our preparation and support system, and the determination to see our goals through.

I insisted. "I know where the peak is. I came prepared. And the top is that way. I'm going to the top." My guide and I debated the issue, but I'd looked into the matter before arriving. I knew Nelion wasn't the peak, and the Gates of Mist would be difficult, but I was determined to see this through to its conclusion. Eventually, my guide agreed to proceed, though he was visibly concerned about the additional risks.

While "walking on clouds" is often used to describe a feeling of euphoria, in this case, walking through the dense, wet fog felt more like a blindfolded trek through a damp, chilling maze. It turns out walking *on* clouds is very different from walking *through* one. My visibility was at a minimum, to the point that I could only plan my path 10 feet at a time. But, as in life, obstacles can be overcome with persistent resolve and expert guidance. I wasn't settling for anything less than the summit. We traversed the thick curtain of mist for hours and wove through the final ridgelines. I dug deep and kept a keen eye, and soon I reached the pinnacle of my journey, trusting my footing and closely following the guide's lead.

As we neared the end of our hours-long traverse through the mist, the air grew thinner, and my heart raced—I could feel we were close. Finally, with one last strenuous push, we emerged onto the peak, the second-highest summit in Africa. Much like in life, the journey wasn't always straightforward, and I had to fight my way through social and physical barriers, but with resilience and perseverance through the hardships, it had all been worth it. I wish I could say the view was one of sprawling vistas, verdant mountains, and sweeping plains, but it was this: I couldn't see 3 feet in front of me. Anticlimactic except for the profound surge that swelled within me, an affirmation that this—the towering heights and constant challenge of my limits—was precisely what I wanted.

I learned that the journey isn't always picturesque. In Kenya, it involved crossing tumultuous terrains while steeped in mist. It included challenges of deeply ingrained biases and questions of my motivation and competence. I'd had to push past barriers—physical exhaustion, dwindling supplies, disagreements with my guide, and my creeping self-doubt—to break records. Yet, as I stood at the top of the peak, gripping the photograph of my family tightly, the sense of achievement was so profound and hit me with such a force that every stumbling stone seemed to crystallize into a single diamond truth: it had been worth every struggle.

BE BREAKPROOF: HOW TO SET YOURSELF UP FOR SUPPORT

1. **Recognize Interdependence.** Humans are interdependent, especially when one is embarking on a challenging journey. Building and maintaining a strong support system can be invaluable, whether it's your family, friends, colleagues, or even strangers who believe in your cause. These systems can provide you with critical guidance, emotional reassurance, and expert knowledge when you face challenging moments or need advice, and they can hold you accountable to your goals, making your journey smoother and more informed.

2. **Find Motivation in Helping Others.** Sometimes motivation doesn't have to come solely from personal growth. Helping others can be a springboard for our development, as it was for me when I agreed to deliver an ambulance and feminine hygiene products to Kenya. This outward focus can sustain your energy and sense of purpose when your motivation might wane.

3. **Leverage Social Media for Support.** While initially reluctant, I shared my journey via social media, allowing others to support my cause and stay updated on my progress. This visibility can generate emotional and practical support from a vast network. It can connect you with like-minded individuals who share your passion and can offer wisdom and encouragement.

4. **Turn Negativity Into Fuel.** Negative comments or critiques can be turned into motivation to prove the naysayers wrong, much like I did. Rather than letting negative feedback or adversity weigh you down, use it as fuel to improve, persevere, and reach your goals. This approach can help you strengthen your resolve, build resilience, and turn your critics into unwitting catalysts for success. It's about reframing your mindset to see challenges as opportunities.

5. **Advocate for Yourself.** Standing up for one's rights, as I did in my interactions with the local guides, is crucial. While respecting the local culture is essential, asserting your rights and needs is equally important. Make your objectives clear and negotiate when necessary.

6. **Accept and Provide Help, Even in Unusual Circumstances.** I employed twenty men to help me on the climb, not necessarily because I needed all of them for the climb itself, but because they needed the employment. This shows that accepting and providing help can sometimes benefit both the giver and the receiver, underscoring the mutual nature of support systems.

7. **Be Resilient and Stay Focused on Your Goal.** Staying focused on the ultimate goal and pushing through challenges and obstacles can help build resilience and determination. Remember why you started, and let that purpose guide you through the difficult times.

8. **Do Your Research Beforehand.** Before you embark on your journey—be it a hike, a new job, or any life-altering decision— make sure you are thoroughly prepared. Like I knew the actual peak was beyond Nelion, you, too, should know your ultimate destination. Use all available resources to learn about potential challenges and how to navigate them. This preparation will help you argue your case when your journey is questioned and make you more confident in facing adversity. Know the facts and risks and have a Plan B (and C) in place.

9. **Trust in Your Guidance but Keep Your Autonomy.** I relied on a guide to help me through the perilous journey, but when we disagreed on the destination, I stood my ground. In life, it's important to seek guidance from mentors and advisers, but ultimately, you need to trust your instincts and judgment. Do not shy away from standing up for your goal when necessary. Guidance should serve as a support, not dictate your every move. Keep your autonomy, and remember that your journey is unique to you. Your path may diverge from the advice given, and that's okay.

10. **Value Your Personal Growth Over External Validation.**
When you finally achieve your goal, it may not look like what
others perceive as success. I reached the summit but couldn't
see anything due to the dense fog. Nevertheless, I felt the
surge of achievement. This implies that success should be
measured by your personal growth and the effort you've put
into the journey, rather than the applause or recognition you
receive from others. Celebrate your victories based on your
benchmarks, even if they don't fit into conventional norms.
Remember, it's your journey and your triumph. Hold your head
high, knowing your achieved growth is more significant than
any external accolade.

FINDING A SYSTEM YOU SUPPORT
AND THAT SUPPORTS YOU

Everyone needs a support system when reaching for their goals. No one is exempt from needing help, no matter how big or small the goal is. The key is to find a system that not only supports you, but one you can contribute to as well. Offering help is a give-and-take deal. That's how communities are built, and everyone is made better by one person achieving their goals and then, in turn, helping others achieve theirs. A support system could include mentors, friends, family, professional networks, or community groups, each of whom can provide different types of encouragement, resources, and guidance.

Maintaining a strong support system is as crucial as building one. Regularly express your gratitude to those who assist you, keep them updated on your progress and, when possible, offer your support in return. This creates a positive, reciprocal relationship that lasts beyond achieving a single goal. And when you reach your goal, consider how you can give back to your support system. Perhaps this means mentoring someone else who is now where you started, or volunteering your time or expertise in a way that aligns with your skills and passions.

Support systems come together with carefully identified people who share your vision, are genuinely invested in your success, are dependable during the highs and lows, exercise courage to give feedback on your blind spots, and have your back at every turn.

I've learned the importance of these support systems in some of the most dangerous and difficult-to-reach places on earth. From my time climbing Mt. Kenya, I learned how to best offer support, accept help, and identify valuable systems that are universally applicable. As you read this book, I hope you'll be able to see your own goals reflected in mine, and learn how being breakproof and resilient is contingent on the circle of friends, mentors, guides, and supporters you surround yourself with. Just as I relied on my guide while climbing Mt. Kenya, consider who in your life can act as a "guide" in your endeavors—someone who has navigated similar challenges and can offer valuable insights.

Despite the twenty men I paid to set me up at the base of the mountain and the single guide leading me up the climb, I didn't actually have a great support system on this expedition, highlighting the importance of developing one. The grueling climb on this mountain became the genesis for my clarity about the need for a strong, aligned support system. A profound, sometimes painful, epiphany fundamentally shifted my approach to climbing and life. Support systems come together with carefully identified people who share your vision, are genuinely invested in your success, are dependable during the highs and lows, exercise courage to give feedback on your blind spots, and have your back at every turn. To build this kind of support system, start by identifying individuals who have shown genuine interest in your journey. Reach out to them, be clear about your vision, and invite open, honest communication. Nurture these relationships regularly, through both the good times and the bad.

It's up to you, the dreamer, to make that first move and ask for help.

Ask for Help

More often than not, the foundations of a support system start with you. While the efforts of others are always helpful (such as my friend reaching out to deliver an ambulance), relying on someone else to get the process started will only delay your efforts to become breakproof in reaching your goals.

Our goals are more often self-centered. After all, they're *our* goals. *We* should be most excited, invested, and active in seeing them through to a successful end. But you will always need a system of support. Most people don't spend their days looking for ways to help others, asking everyone they talk to if they can help make their dreams come true. It's up to you, the dreamer, to make that first move and ask for help. It's common to fear rejection or feel like a burden when asking for help, but remember that people often appreciate the opportunity to lend a hand when asked. Starting with a simple noncommittal question such as "Do you have any advice on...?" can open the door to assistance without putting the other person on the spot.

You can also make it easier for others to offer you help by being as clear and specific in your goals as possible. Communicate your vision clearly, outline the steps you think are necessary, and identify the areas where you need assistance the most. It's one of my many rules of life: The more specific you are in your goals, the more likely others are to offer help. For example, if your goal is to "run faster than you ever have," you may not have people lining up to provide their expertise. The vagueness of the goal makes it more difficult for others to find a helpful avenue to help. On the other hand, if your goal is to "run a marathon," others are far more likely to help. If they've run a marathon before, they may offer suggestions on how to train, what to eat, or how to pace yourself. If they haven't, maybe they know someone who has. But you could even get more specific with your goal, such as "running a marathon in under four hours." Now, others know what your goal is and what aspects of the goal are most important to you. The greater detail you provide in your goals, the easier it is for others to immediately see how they might be able to help. When communicating your goals, consider sharing why they matter—not just to you but to your community or even the world. People are often more motivated to support goals that have a clear, positive impact beyond personal achievement.

Your potential goal of starting a small business will take loads of your free time away, but not all of it. It's important that you ask for help when getting things started. Yes, you may want to have your hands in all the little details, but assembling a team will help ease the burden on your shoulders and help operations run smoothly. This team might include a mentor with business experience, a partner who complements your skills, or even a group of friends willing to volunteer their time for some initial tasks. And you'll more than likely need to be the one to ask for help. When assembling your team, look for individuals who share your vision and values and bring diverse skills and experiences. A complementary team can constructively challenge your ideas, offer fresh perspectives, and fill gaps in your skillset, making your business more resilient and adaptive.

It's important to remember that not everyone you ask for help will be able or willing to assist. Don't let a no discourage you. Thank those who decline for their time, and keep seeking support that aligns with your vision. And while external support systems are invaluable, don't overlook the importance of supporting yourself. Regular self-care, positive self-talk, and setting aside time for relaxation and reflection are all vital components of a holistic support system.

Offer Help

Still, wouldn't it be great if others did offer to help unprompted? You wouldn't have to be coy about asking for help and wondering if they think your goal is worth it. Sharing our goals is scary, let alone asking for help with them. That's where the other half of "making the first move" comes into play: Be the first to *offer* help. Taking the initiative to help others is empowering and can set a positive tone in your community.

Let's take the previous example of starting a small business. Imagine that while your small business is just getting started, you notice your friend has just started a new job. While they're excited to work in their position, they've found it challenging to navigate and adapt to all the new expectations and procedures that come with working for a new company.

You could get away with not extending help to your friend very easily. After all, you're bogged down with all the responsibilities of your own business, and you wouldn't want to stretch yourself too thin. You're chasing your own goals! You don't have time for anyone else. But even when you are busy with your pursuits, extending a helping hand can be incredibly rewarding. This is where offering a simple gesture of support, such as sending a message to check in or offering to share your own experiences, can make a significant impact. However, extending help to others builds your community and broadens your horizons. While helping your friend with their new job, you may gain insight into how to solve one of the issues you're facing in your own business. For instance, while advising your friend on communication strategies, you might come across a new technique that could improve your team interactions. And even if you don't, the kindness and generosity you sow now will reap benefits for you and others around you later, making for a better community for everyone around you, including yourself.

Even if you can only help in small ways—listening to your friend vent, going on a walk to help unwind after a long day, offering to run an errand, making a meal, or simply sending a thoughtful message—your friend will appreciate any help they receive. It may not seem like much, but these small gestures are often the most meaningful. They help to foster trust and build relationships that are reciprocal in nature. Take that first step in offering help; you'll see it return to you quickly.

Be hyperaware of those friends, family members, business associates, vendors, clients, etc., that might be suffering in silence and, for whatever reason, don't have the confidence or skills to ask for your help. This means regularly checking in with people in your life, asking deeper questions during your interactions, and cultivating an attitude of empathy and openness. Work on this. Improve. Expanding and growing: That's the key to becoming breakproof.

Understand Power Structures in Support Systems

When climbing Mt. Kenya, I hired a guide to make sure I made it to the top safely. To clarify, my top, not his top. He was expertly trained and had completed this and similar climbs multiple times. That's one tally mark for "systems that help." However, the aspect within that system that hindered my progress was the extreme patriarchal attitude within the community; I was often met with surprise that a woman would undertake such a climb, and I felt that I was sometimes not taken as seriously as a male climber might have been. That attitude extended to my guide and the gentlemen who carried my equipment to the mountain base. Kenya wasn't the first place I had experienced prejudice because I was a woman in a "man's sport," and it certainly wouldn't be the last. Whenever I faced it, I had to fight against that attitude to successfully summit the mountain, Mt. Kenya included.

But I also needed to understand the layers beyond that. Taking it from my guide's perspective, the money coming in from adventure tourism fed them and kept the lights on. That's a system that benefited them. However, the kinds of tourism from Europe and North America also came with cultural differences that, if not addressed and understood correctly, could lead to misunderstandings or unintentional offenses. These cultural differences threatened to cause more disturbances than peaceful interactions. When navigating my conversations with my guide, I had to keep in mind how those power structures might be affecting him and remain courteous and understanding. I had to stand up for myself and be empathic, asserting my worth and capability as a female climber while respecting and understanding his experiences and the cultural context in which he operates. This required active listening, open dialogue, and a willingness to learn and adapt.

No matter where you live or what system you operate in, there are parts that help and parts that hinder. Each aspect of a system is like a rock, and you need to find which work as stepping stones and which are stumbling stones. For instance, a stepping stone might be a local mentor who understands the nuances of the environment. In contrast, a stumbling stone could be an ingrained cultural bias that dismisses your capabilities. Understanding these aspects involves self-awareness and social awareness, recognizing the implicit biases, privileges, and systemic barriers in various environments. To develop self-awareness, regularly reflect on your reactions and emotions in various situations, build social awareness, engage in open dialogue with people from different backgrounds, and actively educate yourself on the histories and norms of other cultures. By utilizing the stepping stones and avoiding the stumbling stones, you'll become more breakproof and increase your chances of success. This process also involves continuous reflection and self-improvement, allowing you to better navigate systems that may be flawed or prejudiced yet unavoidable. In these instances, understanding when to challenge the system, when to adapt to it, and when to seek alternatives becomes critical to moving forward in a way that aligns with your values and goals. Ask yourself: "Is challenging this system likely to lead to meaningful change, or will it put me at unnecessary risk? Can I maintain my integrity while adapting to this system? Are there alternative paths that align more closely with my values?"

When in Doubt, Take the Lead

Constantly analyzing the effectiveness and challenges associated with your support systems can sometimes be jarring, even paralyzing. Which system is working? Which do I resist? How do I resist? Is it worth the fight, or should I go along with it and hope it gets me to my destination? By "systems," I mean the structures, norms, and relationships that shape our pathways, whether familial expectations, workplace cultures, or societal norms.

Every situation is different, and it can be challenging to give a blanket statement that will work no matter what. However, what's worked repeatedly for me is one mantra: When in doubt, take the lead. When the path is unclear, and it feels like the systems around you are conspiring to make you quit, that's when it's time to step up and take the lead. Being breakproof doesn't mean you won't face obstacles; it means taking charge when you do. And further, being breakproof doesn't mean you're always taking the lead. Sometimes you may find others exhibiting confidence and competence, which gives you a break from being the leader. Becoming breakproof does not mean you are always in charge or in control.

Becoming breakproof does not mean you are always in charge or in control.

Climbing Mt. Kenya, I had to check and double-check not only each step I took but what to say and how to act around others. I needed support. That was certain. But how could I get that support most readily? How could I make supporting me in my goals attractive and even beneficial to others? And if I couldn't make it beneficial for all parties, how could I most diplomatically get what I needed? Could I offer to share my knowledge about a particular aspect of climbing in exchange for guidance in another area? Could I candidly talk with my guide about our respective goals for this expedition and find common ground?

In my experience, taking the lead was how I put my money where my mouth was. I could advocate for myself, my needs, and my goals, but until I backed it up with action, no one would have any reason to walk (or climb) with me. Keep in mind, that didn't always mean taking the physical lead for me on Mt. Kenya. Your guide will almost always know the path ahead better than you because they're trained to deal with these situations. However, I found times when taking the lead was in my best interest. I had more experience traversing snow and ice on mountains, so I was called on to take the lead several times.

When chasing your goals, the systems surrounding you may discourage you. Whether it's a cynic decrying your efforts outright or something subtle like a friend making a passive comment, you'll sometimes feel like quitting is the best way to go. Take the lead, blaze your trail, and summit your mountain.

// REFLECTION QUESTIONS

1. How can helping others achieve their goals help you progress
    on your own? What's one way you've seen in previous pursuits
    how offering assistance came back to help you in the end? For
    instance, have you ever helped a colleague on a project and
    later found them willing to return the favor when you needed it?

    _____

    _____

    _____

    _____

    _____

2. The goals we're striving for may come with "good enough" points
    along the way. How can you persist to your ultimate destination
    when the temptation to settle for "close to the summit" arises?
    What strategies or reminders could you implement to motivate
    yourself to keep pushing forward?

    _____

    _____

    _____

    _____

    _____

    _____

3. Whom can you ask for help in achieving your goals? What is the first move you can make to ask for assistance? Could it be a direct conversation, sending an email, or perhaps joining a group or club related to your goal?

_____

_____

_____

_____

_____

_____

_____

_____

4. In the systems of people around you, which parts are most beneficial to your progress? Which parts might be getting in the way? How can you engage more with the beneficial components and minimize or alter the negative ones?

_____

_____

_____

_____

_____

_____

_____

5. What can you do to increase the joy you're experiencing along the way to your goal, not just the joy in achieving the goal itself? Could this be celebrating small wins, finding a community of like-minded individuals, or integrating your goal-related activities into your daily routine in a way that brings you satisfaction?

_____

_____

_____

_____

_____

_____

_____

CHAPTER 5

NAVIGATE THE
MESSY MIDDLE

MT. TOWNSEND

This chapter unfolds the intertwined tales of two mountains: Mt. Townsend in Australia and Sumantri in Papua, central figures in the contentious debate over the true Seven Second Summits. Two prominent mountaineers—Oliver Preston, a British veteran climber with over three decades of experience, and Isabelle Fontana, an emerging alpinist from Switzerland—disagreed over which of these two peaks deserved the title of the Second Summit. Preston passionately believed Mt. Townsend held the rightful title due to its geographical location, while Fontana argued for Sumantri's recognition because of its greater altitude and the very technical challenges it presented. Both had significant followings in the mountaineering community, and their public disagreements on forums and in articles intensified the debate. Their individual narratives, while divergent, symbolize the deep-seated passions and nuances that mountain climbing evokes. Faced with this dispute, I had to make a critical decision amid geopolitical challenges: Which of these contending mountains would I climb to set a world record? This choice extended beyond a physical ascent, requiring me to navigate a complex and passionate debate within the mountaineering community. The contrasting perspectives surrounding these two mountains vividly illustrate life's unpredictability, highlighting the challenges we encounter when striving for success in a world of competing definitions and ever-changing landscapes.

In New South Wales, Australia, Mt. Townsend stands as a stark contrast to the other mountains on the list of the Seven Second Summits. At 2,209 meters (7,247 feet), it's notably shorter than its towering cousins, like Mt. Tyree in Antarctica. Climbing Mt. Townsend, though, is akin to navigating a small ski resort, with a vertical gain akin to the largest chair lift's 1,840 feet. While its elevation might seem modest and the terrain predictable, the mountain held surprises for us. We didn't anticipate winter clinging so tenaciously, turning what should have been a snowless climb into a snowy expedition. Dense fog hampered visibility, and we post-holed for a taxing mile. And yet, for all its challenges, it's a mountain I'd feel comfortable introducing to my children, if not for its length. This journey underscored a truth: challenges are not solely about magnitude but also about unpredictability and adaptability. Each mountain, no matter its height, tests our perseverance and resilience.

I embarked on my Mt. Townsend journey only after attempting Sumantri on Papua. Sumantri stands at a much more commanding 4,870 meters (15,978 feet). The island of Papua is split in half: the east side is controlled by Papua New Guinea as part of the nations of Oceania; the west side is under the government of Indonesia, part of Asia. Therefore, Sumantri sits on an island that is geographically part of Oceania but in a nation that's part of Asia, which has caused no small stir among the mountaineering community. The island's divide reflects the ideological divide among climbers concerning the actual geographical boundaries that define these Second Summits.

Clear as mud, right?

The Least Messy Time Frame

For an American, visiting Papua—especially West Papua—is fraught with danger due to a three-way power struggle over the world's largest gold mine. With American corporations owning the mine, any American becomes a potential pawn amid the conflict between Indonesia, Papua New Guinea, and West Papua's locals. I should clarify that my purpose as a climber isn't to take sides in this political mire. While I've simplified the situation, it's these complexities that deterred my Sumantri ascent. The island has been a nexus of political tensions due to its split governance and the abundant natural resources it harbors. Historically, the indigenous tribes of West Papua have sought greater autonomy or outright independence from Indonesia, leading to tensions and periodic outbreaks of violence. This volatile mix of regional politics, international interests, and indigenous rights has made Papua a hotbed for conflict, making any expedition to its peaks fraught with risks far beyond the usual mountaineering hazards.

I had specific reasons to attempt Sumantri at that time: ensuring I climbed both disputed summits and capitalizing on the rare safety window during President Biden's presence. While President Biden's Papua visit was unrelated to my journey, his presence and the ensuing G20 Summit meant heightened security, a silver lining for my attempt.

Despite all precautions, the inherent risks of being in West Papua weighed on me because of my role as a parent. I flirted with death just setting foot on the island. Yes, I believe in setting an example of courage and determination for my children, building their confidence, grit, and perseverance, and instilling in them the audacity to take on whatever they want in life—a version of my audacious goal. Yes, I recognize that journalists, politicians, activists, adventurists, explorers, discoverers, members of the military, and countless other movers and shakers pursue noble pursuits in a landscape fraught with danger. Yes, I was setting a world record.

But I was still terrified to die.

And so, it was with enormous contemplation and care and with every security protocol possible that I attempted this most dangerous summit. I traveled in an armored vehicle and slept in a motel with barred windows, situated in a secure compound, still a helicopter ride away from the base of this mountain.

Our bid to summit faced a perfect storm of challenges: rebel-controlled terrains and significant seismic activity, including an earthquake so far-reaching that it caused a volcano to erupt *in Hawaii*, more than 6,000 miles away. The chain reaction from the tectonic plates shifting had caused a natural disaster on the other side of the Pacific Ocean. The earth beneath us was hellbent against this climb. In addition, Papua's history is fraught with tales of active cannibalistic tribes, an unsettling backdrop to the already tense political climate. In hindsight, recent tourist fatalities linked to these tribes were likely the turning point in my decision to abandon the climb; I wasn't ready to roll the dice.

With each challenge, I couldn't help but ask myself, "Was I sane to even attempt this?" While each obstacle was formidable on its own, collectively they formed an insurmountable barrier.

Eventually, for my safety, I figured out a way off the island, catching a flight to Bali. As I retreated from West Papua, I felt a sweet sense of relief tinged with the bitterness of defeat. Additionally, this experience gave me a new perspective on success. It's not just about reaching your goals but reaching your goals *safely*. What's not a reasonable choice is someone with bravado luring people into situations that can be prevented with good judgment and by not taking careless risks. As the plane touched down in Bali, I felt a profound weight lift off my shoulders; for the first time in what felt like an eternity, I could breathe freely again. Rather than the frustration or disappointment one might expect after such a harrowing ordeal, I felt a profound sense of relief—a clear sign, in retrospect, that turning back was the right decision. Surviving the ordeal and making a hasty exit from the island had drained me.

But I wasn't going home just yet. Instead, I was setting my sights on a new target: the resolute and stoic Mt. Townsend in Australia, which, though physically less imposing than Sumantri, was waiting to test my resolve in a new way.

Might as Well Try

Mt. Townsend was more than just another climb. It was meant to be my grand finale, a triumphant moment with my children cheering by my side. As the smallest and most straightforward of the Second Summits, I envisioned flying to the sun-kissed coasts of Australia with all my kids and finishing this journey together. They had been my rock and my biggest cheerleaders throughout each climb; every time I reached a challenging point, the thought of their encouraging words and the memories of their tight hugs kept me going. I figured I could complete Townsend with them and have them be a vital part of my journey.

After the crushing disappointment of my failed attempt at Sumantri, hidden in the heart of Papua's range, I also wanted to prove to myself that I could conquer at least one of these mountains. After the harrowing challenges I faced at K2, with its biting cold and treacherous paths, conquering Dykh-Tau immediately afterward had been a testament to resilience. This felt similar—another opportunity to rebound from a negative experience. Just like in life, learning from our past struggles and climbs can help inform us how to bounce back quickly when faced with similar challenges.

While my heart yearned for redemption, there was also a practical side to attempting Mt. Townsend. I'd flown to the other side of the world for Sumantri, and after that heartbreak, it would be a waste if I flew back without having even attempted one of these summits. But life, much like mountain climbing, is rarely a straight path. It's about navigating the unforeseen, adjusting the sails when winds change direction, and finding light in unforeseen detours. Plus, given its reputation, I could evaluate if this was the kind of mountain my kids could handle climbing. If the climb seemed manageable, I would hold off reaching the summit, planning to return later and share the experience with all of them. Despite being a challenge, it wouldn't be that long of a detour anyway. The climb can be completed in a single day—no base camp, no tents. Just the gear you hiked in with and the will to reach the top.

So I booked a flight to Sydney and dived into research. Being close neighbors, the trail to Mt. Townsend is the same as Kosciuszko's, Australia's highest peak. Interestingly, Mt. Towsend adjoins a ski resort, and being the early bird I am, I made it to the chair lift almost an hour before it opened. The trail to the summit weaves its way through the lively lower-level ski resort. Here, a rather unconventional start awaits mountaineers—the opportunity to take a chair lift right up to the summit of the ski resort. From there, one can begin hiking the mountains behind the resort. These mountains, in contrast to the more rugged terrains often encountered in mountaineering, are largely flat with only slight elevation gains for the most part. This unique blend provides an incomprehensible comfort, riding a ski lift to kickstart an expedition. I did not participate in that comfort, because I was there an hour before it opened. Determined (or perhaps just impatient), I chose to hike up under the ski lift, following the shadow of the moving chairs above, arriving at the top just as the first chair lift of hikers did. As I trudged uphill, watching the chairs glide effortlessly overhead, I felt a twinge of regret. That day, under the gaze of the mountain, the value of accepting help and embracing modern conveniences hit home. Rather than pushing ahead, I could have waited and saved my energy to make it just as far in about the same amount of time. In our journeys, we must recognize and embrace the tools available to us instead of shouldering unnecessary burdens.

It's about navigating the unforeseen, adjusting the sails when winds change direction, and finding light in unforeseen detours.

If I could offer one piece of advice from my Mt. Townsend journey to my younger self, it would be this: Take advantages when they're provided to you. Since I can't go back in time to tell that to young Jenn, I'll pass it on to you. Life will always present its challenges, just as mountains have steep ascents. But intertwined within these are opportunities—the chair lifts, the helping hands—waiting to be recognized and embraced. Seek them out and let them elevate your journey. They might make the climb a bit easier.

Through the Slush and Mud

In the expanse of Mt. Townsend, devoid of its forested base at higher elevations, there are no trees to carry any scent. The landscape is surprisingly straightforward; it's essentially a walk. However, unlike the serene, snow-free vistas some might expect, we encountered a different scenario: the ground beneath us was covered in a layer of snow, not the soft, fluffy kind, but more like freezer-burned ice cream, resulting from a freeze-thaw cycle. This transformed the snow into sharp, icy pebbles, making our journey feel akin to wading through a foam pit at a trampoline park, but with a cutting edge to each step. While it wasn't quite waist-deep, the snow often reached our midthighs, making movement laborious and, at times, painful. Though the terrain wasn't necessarily challenging, the journey was long. A perfect route would clock in at 14 miles, but with weather hindrances and navigational missteps, we found ourselves trekking for 16 miles. This distance, particularly in such conditions, is not ideal for a young child, such as a ten-year-old, to tackle in a single day and remain in good spirits.

To make matters worse, the snow had created an environment that was altogether unforgiving. I'd climbed in snow plenty of times before in much colder climates, which are challenging in their own right. Unlike my previous climbs in cold conditions, Mt. Townsend had a unique challenge: warm temperatures turned the snow into a hazardous mix of ice on top and slush beneath. Each step was deceptive, and soon we found ourselves wading hip-deep in this treacherous blend. To move forward, you must start post-holing, lifting your leg out of the slush and breaking the ice again. It's an endurance exercise that makes even the shortest hike feel endless. In essence, you are covered in snow somewhere between your knee and waist on each step, and have to lift your leg up and out and repeat this nearly fifteen thousand times. Each of those steps, which I meticulously counted, felt like a test of will.

Although I cursed the terrain, I had to remind myself what I'd just come from on Sumantri. Considering the dangers I'd just faced, like the risk of encountering local tribes with aggressive reputations, I'd choose the snow wade any day. Sometimes life offers us two challenging paths; you must decide which is less daunting and be grateful for it.

Across the Seven Second Summits, Mt. Logan in Canada was, by degrees of magnitude, my most challenging. Comparably, Mt. Townsend was the easiest. Do not confuse easiest with easy. But I think it's important to share that there were some small gifts afforded to me along this expedition, and I'm grateful to have summited this mountain in a single day. It's funny to note that of these fifteen thousand steps, two thousand of them involved my photographer climbing down without a shoe because while we were post-holing down, one of his shoes got stuck in the sloshy snow. When it was finally retrieved, it was drenched, the warmth from his foot having caused any snow crystals inside to melt, creating a squelching mess that, honestly, was so absurd all you could do was laugh it off. When he tried to put it back on, he lost grip of it, and we watched together as it slid the rest of the way down the mountain. He survived, with no frostbite, no worse for the wear. This humorous incident with my photographer's shoe became a lighthearted reminder that, amid the grueling challenges, there are moments of unexpected levity on these climbs. Not every moment of this expedition was life or death; some were incredulous, hilarious, joyful, exhilarating, peaceful even.

Sometimes life offers us two challenging paths; you must decide which is less daunting and be grateful for it.

Becoming breakproof—building the mental resilience and agility necessary for enduring these demanding expeditions—doesn't mean you're always at the precipice of death or triumph. It means you're constantly growing and expanding, and the summit to Mt. Townsend afforded me the precious opportunity to realize the importance of seizing opportunities when they arrive, even when serendipitous. Remember, I set out to climb a mountain in Papua and ended up being forced out of the country Sydney Bristow-style (for you non-TV thriller people, that's Jennifer Garner's character in *Alias*), and hopped the flight to Australia with no notice, adding Mt. Townsend to my list within forty-eight hours. Sometimes becoming breakproof requires the agility and nimbleness necessary to pivot at a moment's notice.

As I trudged through the deceptive snow on Mt. Townsend, I found myself in the "messy middle" of my journey. It's that space where:

- You're inexplicably losing momentum, and you don't exactly know why.

- The adrenaline is gone, your frustration level is up, and you can either give up or try a little bit harder and longer.

- You're seriously questioning why you're on this journey and considering bailing or lowering your expectations.

- You don't know when the end is in sight. You don't know how much farther you must go or whether something lurks in the corner.

The messy middle is where dreams go to die. It's the sometimes-silent unseeable quagmire everyone sees themselves in but rarely names or recognizes. This might be the most crucial part of this book, so please check in for a moment. The messy middle is deceptive, like quicksand. It looks just like any other stretch, but once in, challenges pull you deeper, subtly and slowly. This is where most people quit and give up becoming breakproof. This is your moment of truth. We all face it. Heck, I faced it countless times on my journey to summit these seven mountains, and also as a parent, an entrepreneur, a friend, and a human just surviving everyday setbacks and challenges life throws at you. You're bound to face your own "messy middle," and when you do, remember these insights to navigate through:

Becoming breakproof doesn't mean you're always at the precipice of death or triumph. It means you're constantly growing and expanding.

- **Expect the mess.** If you go into it expecting something messy to happen, you'll have the mental resilience to take it on headfirst when you get to that point. Just as I had anticipated unpredictable weather on Mt. Townsend, expecting challenges in life sets you up with a resilient mindset.

- **Let go of your emotions.** Reconnect to logic and create a structure for yourself. Everyone needs a bridge, a rope, or a stick to pull themself out of their quicksand.

- **Call it what it is.** Acknowledge it. Name it. Speak out loud about your struggle. Call your support system. Tell them you're struggling. You're second-guessing. Optimize everything that's going well and openly share your fears.

Facing and navigating through your own "messy middle" is a profound step toward becoming breakproof—toward growing and persevering, no matter how insurmountable the obstacles may seem.

BE BREAKPROOF: HOW TO NAVIGATE THE MESSY MIDDLE

1. **Adapt to Changing Conditions.** The climb of Mt. Townsend demonstrated the importance of adaptability. Regardless of meticulous planning, unexpected circumstances can emerge, and the ability to adjust plans accordingly becomes crucial. In the face of rapidly changing weather patterns, I had to abandon the planned path and opt for a safer, alternative route.

2. **Persevere in the Face of Difficulty.** Overcoming unpredictable weather conditions and unforeseen terrain difficulties during the climb showcased my ability to persist. Sometimes the most significant challenges aren't the most obvious ones. Enduring through snowstorms and icy trails, I learned to brace myself mentally and physically for unexpected situations. Always anticipate the unexpected and be prepared for it.

3. **Stay Aware of Your Surroundings.** The risky situation around Sumantri highlighted the significance of situational awareness. In complex and precarious scenarios, noticing a sudden drop in temperature and adjusting plans preemptively can be lifesaving. Being vigilant about potential risks can be pivotal in determining success or failure.

4. **Recognize When to Stop.** During the Sumantri expedition, I learned that recognizing when to stop is as important as persisting. When a member of our team developed severe altitude sickness, we knew it was time to descend. When conditions become too hazardous, it's crucial to prioritize safety over the mission. People over peaks.

5. **Seize Opportunities to Bounce Back.** After the unsuccessful attempt at Sumantri, the swift success at Mt. Townsend reminded me that recovery often involves acknowledging the setback but quickly refocusing energy on the next achievable goal, seizing new opportunities with optimism.

6. **Use Available Resources Wisely.** My experience with the
    chairlift on Mt. Townsend emphasized the importance of using
    available resources. Don't overlook the "chairlifts" in your
    journey—tools and assistance that can conserve your energy
    and effort.

7. **Value Safety as Success.** While summiting peaks, I realized
    that success isn't just about reaching goals but achieving them
    safely. During a climb where a fellow mountaineer suffered
    a severe injury, I was reminded that it's essential to prioritize
    personal well-being over ambitious endeavors.

8. **Build Resilience Against Unfavorable Conditions.** Climbing
    in slushy snow was a testament to strength. Despite freezing
    temperatures and treacherous footing, I committed to
    continue moving forward, step by step. Standing up to adverse
    conditions and pressing on can often lead to breakthroughs
    and success.

9. **Learn From Past Experiences.** My earlier challenging climb
    at K2 and the subsequent success at Dykh-Tau taught me
    to learn from past struggles and apply that wisdom to future
    challenges. For example, I realized the importance of adequate
    acclimatization and nutrition and carried those lessons into later
    expeditions. This learning is crucial to navigating the "messy
    middle" and swiftly adapting to new circumstances.

10. **Understand the Importance of Help.** I learned the hard way
    not to carry unnecessary burdens. When facing a particularly
    challenging section of Mt. Townsend, I accepted assistance
    from a fellow climber, which was invaluable. Whether it's the
    chairlift up a mountain or tools and help in life, using available
    resources can avoid needless exhaustion and accelerate progress.
    Acknowledging and accepting help saves time and effort and
    enables more effective achievement of goals.

THE MESSY MIDDLE

Life's journey, especially when striving for goals, can seem cluttered and complicated. That's a slightly softer way of saying, "Sounds tough. Get over it." When striving for your goals, you'll have to deal with unexpected roadblocks, convoluted loopholes, and less-than-ideal circumstances. It happens to all of us, but the best of us work through them. Being breakproof, undaunted by setbacks and determined to persevere, is about looking at the messy middle—the challenging and uncertain phase that gets between you and achieving your goals—and not being deterred. While some messes are just too complicated to work through at the time, by relentlessly pushing forward, even when the path is unclear, you inch closer to your dreams and open up avenues you didn't even know existed. Sumantri, with its unforeseen obstacles and impossible-to-navigate political climate, was a mess that grew too big for me to manage. But while I couldn't work through it then, I could adapt to the situation, still score a win, and move forward in my goals.

Drawing from these experiences, when you encounter your own "messy middle," remember that becoming breakproof is your armor; it will help you resist the urge to give up and instead focus on what good you can take from a situation. Below are a few lessons I learned from Sumantri and Mt. Townsend that helped me become more breakproof on and off the mountain.

By relentlessly pushing forward, even when the path is unclear, you inch closer to your dreams and open up avenues you didn't even know existed.

Not Clean, but Clean Enough

Mountaineering is a constant dance of compromises, balancing essential needs against the necessity of maintaining a manageable load. If you pack more clothes—for instance, a down jacket or an extra pair of thermal leggings—you'll be able to adapt to a wider range of climates. However, you're also adding weight to your pack, which will slow you down and tire you out. Consider the steep inclines, slippery terrains, and high altitudes; each ounce matters. The "perfect" amount of clothes to pack doesn't exist; it's about finding the balance between bringing a down jacket for freezing nights and avoiding overpacking that will weigh you down during steep ascents. In life, much like mountaineering, being breakproof doesn't hinge on discovering a one-size-fits-all system. It's about crafting the system best suited for the present goal, understanding that the process may change in a week, a month, or a year when new challenges arise or priorities shift. You're not searching for the immaculate, obstacle-free path ahead, just the one that's clean enough to navigate successfully.

Take my venture to West Papua, for instance. I understood the risks of attempting Sumantri. This wasn't just about the physical challenges of the climb but also the geopolitical and environmental factors of the region. Zooming out to the big picture, I knew completing the Seven Second Summits would be fraught with unpredictable challenges and potential hazards. Yet, if I constantly waited for those rare moments when victory seemed guaranteed, the adventure would remain a mere daydream, and I would be confined to the comfort of my living room.

Being breakproof means seizing imperfect opportunities and making the most of what's presented. Life won't always hand you ideal circumstances, but cultivating a resilient and opportunistic mindset will embolden you to venture out, risk, and persevere.

Yet, this doesn't grant a license for recklessness. There's a discernible difference, a nuanced boundary, between grasping an opportunity and jumping the gun. As I've gleaned from past endeavors and regrets, pausing to evaluate, slowing down, and considering all available options can be the pivotal factor that defines success. Reflect on situations deciding whether to wait for a chair lift, weighing energy conservation against potential time saving. Similarly, you, too, will often be faced with decisions: those that offer immediacy and those that promise efficiency.

To illuminate this further, imagine you're keen on launching a new product in your business. Market trends indicate a growing interest in your product category. An overwhelming surge of enthusiasm might compel you to launch immediately without adequate market research. But recollect past business ventures: Perhaps you've made hasty decisions that backfired due to lack of preparation. Instead of plunging headlong into an immediate launch and potentially facing negative feedback or low sales, consider investing time in comprehensive market research, targeting a well-informed launch later. Alternatively, look for niche markets or pilot test groups to introduce your product, giving you invaluable insights without overcommitting.

Navigating the "messy middle" demands a delicate balance between thorough preparation and unwavering determination. On top of that, understand that sometimes you'll prepare for a mess that never happens, but you'll gain greater insight on how to prepare for the next hurdle. I've taken plenty of clothes on hikes that I never wore and packed water that I never drank. I don't regret the extra baggage because I was prepared for the mess. As you strive to achieve your goals, consider what messes you may run into and learn how to prepare and adjust to them.

This fluidity, this capacity to adapt and recalibrate— this is what it means to be breakproof.

Surprisingly, life has an uncanny knack for throwing curveballs. Your well-laid plans might not always align with the actual hurdles you encounter. Often it's not the anticipated challenges that surface, but your preparation will arm you for the unexpected ones that do. For instance, when starting a business, you may wisely set aside a rainy-day fund or develop strategies to weather the slow season. Circumstances could demand this contingency fund to pay for new equipment instead. Resources earmarked for one purpose might be pivotal in addressing a different challenge. This fluidity, this capacity to adapt and recalibrate—this is what it means to be breakproof: possessing the resilience and flexibility to change your plans as needed without losing sight of your ultimate goals. It's about foresight and adaptability, ensuring that even if the challenges you anticipated don't arise, you're prepared to face the unforeseen storms that inevitably brew.

Ask Forgiveness of Yourself, Not Permission

After discussing the importance of caution, encouraging a bold spirit might seem out of place. But being breakproof is about striking the right balance between risk and caution. When in the messy middle, it's not uncommon to encounter self-doubt; you may find yourself coming up with excuses not to chase your goal, and while some of these doubts might be grounded, others sprout from deep-rooted fears, insecurities, and anxiety. Regardless of the origin of these excuses, they will feel undeniably real to you and hold you back. The imperative question is then: How do you deal with them? Tackle three at a time.

Imagine, once again, that you're launching a new product for your business in the upcoming quarter. You've been planning and developing for months and feel confident about your progress. But suddenly, unforeseen challenges arise: the manufacturing unit reports a delay in delivering essential components. Boom! Hurdle number one! How can you move past it? It would be easy to postpone the launch or cut corners on quality. But instead, you decide to negotiate with an alternative supplier or optimize the production schedule. First hurdle overcome.

The new supplier provides components, but they aren't the exact specifications you initially planned for. Boom! Hurdle number two! How can you get over that? Maybe you could adjust the product design slightly to accommodate these components or work with the supplier to refine the product over time. Second hurdle overcome.

Lastly, your marketing team informs you that a significant industry event, which was pivotal for your product promotion, has been rescheduled. Boom! Hurdle number three! How can you overcome this third obstacle? Perhaps you can focus on digital marketing campaigns or look for other industry events that align with your product launch. Maybe a collaborative promotion with another brand can give your product the visibility it needs. Third hurdle overcome.

At this point, you could very easily have come to a solution. Great! Now you're one step closer to achieving your goal. That's how the three-hurdle system works. After three problems, you usually find a way to keep moving forward.

But what if there are other roadblocks ahead? What if, what if, what if? The key here is to not overthink things. Keep it simple. Find solutions and move on. Once you've overcome the third hurdle, you have enough momentum to keep jumping over obstacles until you've convinced yourself to go for the gold.

When you face a big challenge, breaking it into smaller tasks can help. For instance, consider my "Climb Mt. Everest From Home" challenge. In the Everest Challenge, we break things into 10-feet sections, which is typically the size of someone's staircase in their house. Every time participants walk past it, if they quickly run up and down, it becomes an easy method to add vertical distance to their day and progress toward the 29,029 feet they aim to climb over the course of forty days. Getting to fly around the world and risk life and limb for a goal isn't available to everyone, so I bring that same challenge to others in their own home. But it's more than just teaching people how to climb a mountain; it's teaching resilience and problem-solving skills, fostering a mindset of relentless pursuit. The first and most important piece of this challenge is breaking the task into no fewer than 100 steps. The philosophy is that if you break your one big challenge into the smallest bits possible, it's less daunting to approach it, and you'll come up with fewer excuses to avoid the task. And in the end, even if you only got 50 of the 100 steps done, that's still better than 0 steps. In the end, it encourages growth rather than cultivating excuses.

Often we disguise our hesitations as "asking ourselves for permission," which is essentially making excuses. You're trying to grant yourself permission by seeing if you can hold up to a bit of resistance. But being breakproof extends beyond mere persistence. It's about adapting and finding new ways to stand firm against resistance. If none of these options work, you can always ask yourself for forgiveness. You might not have made it as far as you wanted, but you worked harder at your goal than you would have otherwise. That experience, the progress you did make, is a foundation to build on, not a failure to lament. You're more likely to complete the task because you went into it open to forgiveness rather than shied away, afraid of getting permission.

It's Going to Get Gross; Play in the Mud

When I descended from Mt. Townsend, I'd been navigating through deep snow and icy conditions for hours. The relentless sun, when not obscured by clouds, and our body heat caused the snow around us to melt, ensuring we were perpetually damp. Saying I was soaked wouldn't capture the half of it. On my return to the ski resort, the employees looked on in astonishment.

"Which hike did you do again?" one of them asked me, like I'd emerged from their nightmares.

"Mt. Townsend," I said.

"Oh. Why? Nobody does Townsend. We've had so much snow this year. How did you not get buried up to your necks?"

"Well, I did it. Why do you think I look like this?"

Every path to your goal will contain some mess along the way, but each brings unique opportunities for growth. It's inevitable. But you know what? Do it anyway. The path is gross; get over it. No matter your goal, there is no way to reach it without getting a few grass stains along the way.

But now that you know reaching for goals comes with inevitable messes, you don't have to worry about keeping everything squeaky clean the whole way through. No, your shoes won't be gleaming when you get there, but you'll get there. And this isn't just about climbing mountains. Whether you attempt your goals or not, the mess will always be there. In one form or another, the chaos and the clutter will enter your life. You can either run from it or dive straight in.

The messy middle is where you confront most challenges, refine your approach, and iron out most problems. It's where you revise your speech or identify the most significant liabilities. It's where the problematic cuts and the most extensive changes are made. The messy middle is stuffed with growing pains but results in growth. Don't fear the mess; let it help you get better!

However, not all messes can be overcome in one go. Part of this chapter told the story of my time on Sumantri, which showed that sometimes you just have to wait for a better time to achieve your goal. Sometimes you must turn the other way, knowing that your willingness to engage with the mess has prepared you better for the next challenge or attempt.

By facing the mess, you become more breakproof. The bits and pieces that deterred you will look more like challenges you can tackle, and in no time, you'll find yourself at your summit. You might smell funky, but you'll be at the finish line. You may be tired, but you're that much stronger. Remember, the journey might be messy, but it's through the mess that you grow and emerge victorious. And that ultimately counts—reaching your goals and overcoming the obstacles you faced.

// REFLECTION QUESTIONS

1. In your journey, do emotions like pride, impatience, frustration, or other feelings hinder accepting help? Recall a recent instance where you might have declined assistance. What might you have said no to that you can rethink and allow a helping hand to lift you?

    _____

    _____

    _____

2. Identify your "messy middle." What specific challenges present themselves halfway through your quest to achieve your goal, and what strategies are you employing to navigate them? How do these challenges make you feel, and what lessons are you learning as you confront them?

    _____

    _____

    _____

    _____

3. Consider your current primary objective. Take the goal before you and break it into 10 distinct steps. Now, further dissect each of those steps into 10 more detailed steps. Be thorough and analytical. Get as specific as you need to in order to outline 100 individual steps for this single goal. Reflect on this exercise: How can this structured approach help you tackle larger tasks with renewed confidence and eagerness?

    _____

    _____

    _____

    _____

CHAPTER 6
RECOGNIZE WHEN IT ISN'T YOUR MOUNTAIN

K2

The infamous K2—majestic, treacherous, and unforgiving. The one that got away. The only one of the Seven Second Summits where, on my first attempt, I made the call to turn around. K2—the mountain where I learned the importance of choosing people over peaks.

Standing tall at 8,614 meters (28,251 feet), K2 is a stark and imposing visual on the border of Pakistan and China. An awe-inspiring spectacle for anyone, it is both revered and feared by local citizens and has become a symbol of thrill-seeking and beauty. It is not only the second-tallest mountain in Asia, behind Mt. Everest, but the second-highest mountain in the world, sitting amid the majestic and rugged Karakoram range, which is part of the Pakistan-controlled portion of the Kashmir region.

By many standards, K2 ranks as a more challenging climb than its taller sister Mt. Everest. In fact, in my training and preparation for K2 in 2021, I climbed Mt. Everest to acclimatize and get a sense of the kind of mountain I'd be scaling. In preparing for K2, "acclimatizing" wasn't just about adjusting to the thin, low-oxygen air; it also meant becoming familiar with the starkly different cultural, political, and geographic landscapes. Mt. Everest is in Nepal, and K2 is in Pakistan; those two countries couldn't be more culturally and politically different.

For example, Nepal is primarily Hindu and Buddhist, while Pakistan is predominantly Muslim. Understanding and respecting these cultural differences was essential to my preparation, a different yet equally important form of acclimatization. This broader acclimatization—to the culture, the politics, and the very land itself—plays a crucial role in becoming breakproof and resilient when facing the world's highest peaks. I spent months physically, mentally, and emotionally training.

K2 is difficult enough that, as of my climb in 2022, there have been more people in space (over 580) than there have been on the summit of K2 (around 450). This stark comparison

You're never prepared for the real thing until you're in the thick of it.

highlights the extreme challenges K2 presents to climbers. *National Geographic* has called it a "savage mountain." Why is K2 so much more difficult? Aside from the usual suspects of less commercialization, K2 is steeper than Everest, boasts more climbing features, and has greater exposure. K2 presents a unique set of challenges beyond its steep, icy slopes. The mountain is notorious for its unpredictable weather, prone to sudden and severe storms. Moreover, it sees more rock fall, largely because it doesn't offer as many spaces to house climbers. Limited spots for camps mean that climbers often have to coordinate their movements up the mountain. In 2021, the number of teams on K2 was scant, underscoring the need for larger teams on such massive mountains. However, 2022 saw a surge in climbers, attributed to both the current year's demand and the backlog from 2021. This increased number eased the workload for setting up climbing ropes, but it also heightened the risk. More climbers meant greater rock-fall hazards, and the ropes, frequently running over rocks, became less reliable as they were subject to wear and potential damage. As I ascended, I recorded videos to document the raw and unfiltered moments of the journey. In one heart-stopping video, rocks can be seen pelting my helmet while I steadied my breath, looking into the camera to honor my team and expedition partners—even in the face of danger, we were in this together.

Because of the remote nature of the peak, the rarity of local porters to assist in the climb, and the naturally perilous conditions, I knew I was in for more than a bumpy ride. I had a loyal but small team— including our lead Sherpa guide and several experienced climbers from various countries, each with their unique strengths and skills that they brought to our expedition.

But as in life, so with mountains: You're never prepared for the real thing until you're in the thick of it. More than any other, this climb drove that point home for me. It was a profound teacher. Although I didn't reach the summit then, I walked away with something possibly even more valuable: a profound respect for the mountain and a deeper understanding of my limits and strengths.

The First Ascent

K2 was set to be my third stepping stone on my tour of the Seven Second Summits. Each completed peak wasn't just a checked box or physical achievement but a mental victory over my limitations. Taking on this third mountain would be a giant leap forward, especially since it was among the most difficult. With Ojos del Salado and Mt. Kenya notched into my metaphorical belt, I was prepared to take on a more notorious peak. The terrain and the region offered their fair share of hurdles to overcome, including logistical issues like transportation and a clash of cultures.

Although my first attempt was unsuccessful, it was a pivotal experience. It didn't break me; it reshaped my resolve, making me more determined to return. Unfortunately, those hard-earned lessons were forged in the crucible of life-threatening disasters.

Stumbling Out of the Gate

The challenges of K2 began well before I set foot on its slopes. For context, my flight was canceled. Now, this is different from the inconvenience of a domestic flight cancellation. The implications are massive when a flight from Los Angeles to Islamabad, Pakistan, gets canceled. Trying to find a replacement at the last minute meant my travel expenses increased fourfold. Having meticulously saved and planned for this expedition and others like it over the years, this sudden increase was a harsh blow. Yet, my determination was unwavering, so I made necessary cuts elsewhere in my budget.

The climbing window for K2 is incredibly narrow. My decision to arrive later than the rest of the team due to some cherished moments with my children post-Everest further squeezed my options. But, with resolve, I secured a flight and was soon airborne, keeping my K2 dream alive.

Even after landing in Islamabad, the journey was far from over. Skardu, the gateway to K2, might be a mere forty-five-minute flight away, but flying within Pakistan has its own complications. The towering mountains and their unpredictable weather often lead to canceled flights. Moreover, the limited number of flights and the frequent overbooking of these internal routes add to the logistical nightmare. While it sounds unimaginable, we chose to drive for thirty-six hours, avoiding the uncertainties of internal flights. The journey was far from comfortable: the sweltering heat, an old jeep with a cracked windshield and no air conditioning, and precarious roads with steep drops made each hour feel much longer. To compound matters, safety concerns, including potential kidnapping risks, forced us to stop and wait for daylight at several points.

Reaching Skardu was just another checkpoint. A six-hour drive still separated us from the true beginning of our expedition. And contrary to what you might think, getting to the base of K2 isn't just a matter of lacing up your boots and starting to climb. It demands a 70-mile trek, taking up to a week. This involves crossing fast-flowing rivers, navigating around deep crevasses, and enduring the increasingly thin air as we gained elevation. During this trek, our videographer suffered a deep cut from a boulder slide, a grave concern given our remote location and limited medical supplies. The wound was so severe that we had to improvise, stitching him up with a needle and thread available to us. Unable to walk due to the injury, we had no choice but to send him out on a donkey to ensure his safety.

People Over Peaks

The "people over peaks" principle emphasizes valuing relationships and safety above unbridled ambition. In business, this means ensuring employee well-being takes precedence over pure profit, being attuned to team burnout, and recalibrating your drive to prevent overwhelming others. A successful leader who is breakproof knows how to achieve results with their team today in a way that allows them to continue achieving results with that same team tomorrow.

The climb up K2 is nothing short of a death trap, with rocks often dislodging and plummeting from great heights. Even a tiny pebble, when falling from such a height, can cause serious injury—it can be like a piercing bullet. It'll cut through your coat, and you'll need stitches. And as if the mountain raining down bullets wasn't enough, the depth of knowledge among the porters varied significantly, showing that their expertise and experience were not on par with what's available in Nepal. This disparity in capability, especially in guiding tasks on such treacherous terrain, posed additional risks for our team.

A successful leader who is breakproof knows how to achieve results with their team today in a way that allows them to continue achieving results with that same team tomorrow.

While preparing for K2, many climbers acclimatize on Broad Peak, another nearby 8,000-meter peak. Although not on my initial agenda, I recognized the value in such climbs. But during the ascent, it became clear: time was against us. When we reached the saddle on Broad Peak, it was evident that the ropes were not yet set. There was a significant amount of snow that year, and all the climbers who were working to install the ropes were already exhausted, having faced more work than they had initially anticipated. We were clearly behind schedule. For any significant peak, reaching the summit before 2 p.m. is crucial. Mountains, especially the size of Broad Peak, can generate unpredictable weather patterns. With these challenges ahead and the day wearing on, I voiced my concerns and wanted to turn around, but my team was hesitant to abandon the ascent. Feeling the weight of the situation and willing to descend solo, Rick Allen, a fellow climber from Scotland, volunteered to accompany me. We made the choice together, putting "people over peaks." Continuing to climb could have led to a harrowing and perilous descent in the dark, jeopardizing not only our own lives but also the lives of our support team waiting for us lower on the mountain. It was a life-saving decision placing our safety and well-being over the allure of the summit, reinforcing that no peak, no matter how majestic or sought after, is worth more than the lives and safety of the people climbing it.

As an experienced climber, Rick had come to K2 with his own aspirations: blazing new trails on the mountain, hoping that multiple options would help divert traffic and make the mountain safer for those who attempted it. But in that moment, our decisions converged. His presence and support on the descent were invaluable. Along your journey to reach your goals, you'll come across others whose plans align, and you can encourage each other. Having a fellow climber makes the ascent, and in this case the descent, less difficult and more enjoyable.

Together, we shared our aspirations and motivated each other. Our conversations ranged from swapping stories of our previous climbing expeditions to discussing the intricacies of high-altitude mountaineering. Rick, who had a deep knowledge of mountaineering history, would recount tales of the great climbers of the past, their triumphs and their tragedies. We debated the ethics of climbing, especially in today's increasingly crowded and commercialized high-altitude environment. He shared his insights on developing new routes, emphasizing the balance of innovation and safety. I talked about my children and how they felt about my adventurous, sometimes perilous pursuits. We acknowledged the deep-seated drive that brought us to these peaks and recognized our responsibility to ourselves, our loved ones, and our team to climb smartly and safely. Rich and heartfelt conversations solidified our bond and reinforced our shared philosophy of "people over peaks." In these quiet, profound moments, we were not just climbers; we were friends, mentors, and confidants, united by our respect for the mountains and for each other.

Our choice not to summit Broad Peak proved wise. An accident trapped several climbers in severe conditions, a fate we had evaded by trusting our instincts and experiences. Adapting to current conditions, whether on a mountain or in pursuit of your goals, will often lead you out of danger's path. So you might ask yourself, "When is sticking with your convictions or instincts becoming at odds with being breakproof?" Well, it's simple. If becoming breakproof means you're putting peaks over people, then you probably should check back in with your instincts to realign with the recurring theme of this book, which is people over peaks.

In time, the team put the horrors of Broad Peak behind them, and we attempted K2. Rick and I parted ways, progressing on different routes, hoping to see each other at the summit soon.

The distant rumble of avalanches punctuated the next morning's climb. A call came crackling over my porter's radio. Then another. And another. The frantic chatter alarmed me; the urgency and despair in the voice broadcasting unwelcome news through the radio's static was palpable. Then the porters' expressions said it all: Something terrible had happened.

A devastating avalanche had struck.

One climber was trapped, one was injured, and one was dead.

It was Rick. Rick had died. The avalanche had claimed him among its casualties.

I was stunned.

I'd gotten to know him well on our recent descent. He had been a comforting presence and a fellow voice of reason.

He'd climbed plenty of mountains before this. And now he was dead.

It shouldn't have happened to Rick.

Lost in my shock, I barely registered someone calling my name. "Jenn? Jenn! The team wants to descend. What about you—do you want to continue up?"

No, no, I didn't want to head up the mountain. Not after Rick.

I wanted to be there for my team.

Rick's tragedy brought the mantra I held close, crashing to the forefront of my thoughts. My heart and mouth aligned without hesitation: "People over peaks."

"What about K2?" someone asked. The window was rapidly closing.

My team was in no position physically, mentally, or emotionally to brave the struggle before us. Neither was I.

I shook my head no. And with that, in honor of Rick and in alignment with the values we had shared, I began my descent.

Grump Dump

When I landed in LAX after the tragedy on K2, I realized I needed to decompress before seeing my kids. I understood the importance of processing trauma before involving my closest relationships. When facing world-altering experiences, we must take the time to understand our emotions so that when we share those stories, we pass on wisdom, not trauma. Because I returned to the United States about a week earlier than anticipated, my children were still in summer camp for a few more days. That meant I had time on my own to work through some of what I'd been through.

So I started my "Grump Dump"—a journaling process where I poured out all my negative emotions and experiences without reservation. I wrote about the canceled flight to Pakistan, its financial repercussions, the failure of my contingency plan, the jeep that took us to Skardu, its cracked windshield and defective shocks, the roads with no guardrails and 2,000-foot drops, the torrential downpour, the threat of potential kidnapping, the 70-mile trek to the base of K2, and the storm that engulfed Broad Peak. I wrote about Sandro getting hurt and his expedition ending early; he was supposed to be my bestie on this climb, but he got turned around before base camp. Days that left me exhausted were outlined in detail. I didn't hold back. People that had irked me made the book. Even meals (or the lack thereof) made the cut. Until finally, I faced my sadness. I poured pages for Rick. I let myself get angry, furiously scribbling about how damn unfair it was. Rick respected that mountain. He wasn't reckless; he was one of the most experienced among us. So why him? I raged about the randomness, the utter lack of reason behind it all. Right there in ink, I admitted I felt guilty for still being here when he was not. Writing it all down, I could feel the weight lifting, if just a bit. *It's not fair*, and I let myself feel that through every word I wrote. I spat my unadulterated frustration and loathing onto the pages of that notebook, which absorbed every word.

Then I burned it.

Call it catharsis, overkill, or an over-the-top gesture, I poured my worst into that book and left it for ashes. And it worked.

I was ready to go home.

The Second Ascent

A year after my first heartbreaking attempt at K2, much had changed. I'd summited Dykh-Tau and Mt. Tyree and attempted Mt. Logan once. Each of their open climbing seasons had fit a neat timeline, and I'd kept myself busy and active after my failed summit of K2. Just as in life, setbacks necessitate finding new paths to success. With the varied successful summits under my belt, I felt my energy and determination rising. But atop every other mountain, the echoes of K2 rang in my ears. The season had come back around, and K2 was calling my name.

I was a new person, a new Jenn. I'd learned to be more cautious and how to build a team I could trust. I knew better questions to ask when vetting climbing companies and had a better understanding that not all teams are created equal. I'd developed my strengths and acknowledged where I was coming up short. My determination had become unyielding, but I recognized the importance of assembling a strong team with the right dynamics. Focused on ensuring success for this second attempt, I hired the famous Mingma G, a Nepalese Sherpa that led the first winter ascent up K2. His entire team was very experienced with 8,000-meter peaks. I realized I didn't need to shoulder every responsibility; trusting reliable teammates was vital; it would get me farther.

It's not about how often you fail to summit, but how often you'll climb back up again.

These lessons and newfound traits are universally beneficial, teaching us to grow in areas where we might lack the necessary skills. Taking a more secure and cautious route often leads to a greater chance of success. Unlike my first, this next attempt at K2 would be head-on and unyielding. I would face whatever came my way and make it to the top with a new team that would watch out for me, and me for them.

But the biggest takeaway from my first failure and subsequent preparation for a second attempt? Perseverance. It's not about how often you fail to summit, but how often you'll climb back up again.

I would put myself in the best position to summit K2.

Making a Difference

As I was trying to find the motivation to head back to Pakistan, I learned of a man who, thanks to my sponsorship, could embark on a lifelong career in mountaineering. I chose to help him because he was the one who helped me exit Pakistan the year before. Giving him the opportunity to climb would be a game changer for him, a chance to position himself as a reputable guide in his home country. Few

Pakistanis have summited their country's prized peak; this would set him apart from almost any other guide. He would be set for life.

Likewise, in life, making another attempt at a goal may mean you have different opportunities to help those around you. While achieving your goals is essential, you can only do it with the support of others. In turn, be sure to offer help as you climb your mountains. Making this a priority will get you closer to your goals, help you contribute to the broader world, and make your communities a better place for you and everyone around you.

In hindsight, my initial failure became a catalyst for change. It led me to both alter my frame of mind and climb at a time when I could provide more opportunities for others. The success of this second attempt, which helped others summit, gave new meaning to my first failed attempt. From my previous failure, I came back with a greater resolve to do good, to put people over peaks.

Climbing Through Sickness

The second climb for K2 came with its challenges, but it also came with some helpful surprises. For starters, my confidence in the flight to Skardu had heightened significantly, thus allowing me to avoid the thirty-six-hour "jeep" experience. That had been a once-in-a-lifetime ordeal I didn't want to repeat. The short flight was a game changer that I can't possibly exaggerate. The safety, comfort, and time saved by flying: immeasurable. Likewise, a second try at your goals may clear some previous obstacles.

The push up from base camp also came with its fair share of dangers, but for the most part, it came and went without incident. Even my cameraman Sandro had an easier time up the mountain. This climb was making itself out to be one of the most straightforward of this expedition.

Except for the anthrax.

Yes, I said anthrax.

As things seemed to go smoothly, I faced this unexpected challenge: a deadly bacterium.

It was likely passed on to me from livestock. No, I hadn't been herding sheep so I could have lamb chops for dinner. *What had happened was* donkeys accompanied us on the 70-mile trek to K2, carrying our excess gear. You damned anthrax-infected donkeys! Of course, I had to pet them. Of course, one of those asses sneezed on me.

You cannot make this stuff up.

I didn't know I had contracted anthrax until I returned to the United States. But after the sneezing encounter, every step became a momentous effort as the bacteria sapped me of my strength, and an unrecognizable level of fatigue became my norm—beyond the normal tiredness that results from all-day climbs in high altitudes. For the entire way up, I was in between states of recovery and getting punched in the gut by a bacterial infection I didn't know I had. It was about survival, persistence, and dedication when my body was staging a mutiny—pure, intense pain. I was miserable.

Trying to summit while struggling with a disease mirrors many real-life problems. Often we find ourselves amid a complex project with a deadline to deliver while also dealing with personal hurdles. By not addressing my problem with the care it needed, I placed my goal at risk and was only lucky to achieve it still, picking up the pieces afterward. My anchor was my team. Their support carried me further than I ever could on my own, especially while wrestling with multiple medical challenges.

Striking a balance between a large, flexible team and a skilled, smaller team is essential, especially when navigating technical climbs.

After summiting K2, I rushed back home and went to the hospital at my family's urging, where I received the care necessary to eradicate anthrax from my body. I would have easily succumbed to the disease without quick and deliberate action. How's that for a newspaper headline? "American Woman Summits K2 and Dies From Anthrax Infection."

The antibiotics weren't enough, and "power-through-it Jenn" was ready to try to make it work, but you need lots of help with this infection. In facing anthrax, I realized it's not just about weathering the storm alone but knowing when to seek help. True strength lies not in enduring pain in silence but in the ability to acknowledge our limits and ask for assistance.

Big Teams Make Mountains Safe

In our personal and professional lives, we must surround ourselves with people who can support us when times get tough, much like having the best team during a climb. Just as you need a team to overcome disasters on a mountain, you need your personal "team" to help you navigate life's challenges. The community you foster will help you when times are tough and make the most of when times are good. The kinds of challenges each of us faces are always made easier when the right people are there to help us through them.

When climbing a mountain, just as in a business project or community initiative, having the right people on a climb is vital, and that includes the right *number* of people. Striking a balance between a large, flexible team and a skilled, smaller team is essential, especially when navigating technical climbs. If your small team comes well equipped and has the proper skillset, you can easily traverse the more difficult paths. However, the rule of thumb is maintaining a large enough team to cover whatever disaster may come. You hope no one gets hurt or is put in a dangerous position, but there's little you can do against the wrath of Mother Nature. People get into predicaments. You want enough people around you to help anyone who may need it in those times.

K2's technical and lengthy nature posed a dilemma: opt for a smaller agile team, or a larger one for safety. Safety won out, proving essential for the climb's success. I would not have made it halfway up the mountain without the appropriate team size. Only a few weeks in, we were already at Camp 2, and after a short descent to acclimatize, we decided to push to the summit. The weather hadn't been forgiving, but we'd hunkered down when necessary and made quick advances whenever possible. It wasn't a rapid ascent, but it was an ascent nonetheless. Even on a mountain like K2 that felt antagonistic to me the whole way up, summiting felt like understanding and connecting with the mountain.

On the morning of our final push, anthrax took its toll on me. It demanded resilience, but the encouragement and support from my team were indispensable. K2 had forced me to turn back once, but it couldn't keep me from rising to my feet again. As I would soon learn, with a willingness to face your challenge head-on, you'll surpass even the most treacherous obstacles.

Finally, on a rare clear summit day, I reached K2's peak. The mountain that had once shattered my resolve was now entirely beneath my feet—a mountaineering victory and a testament to my indomitable willpower. Despite earlier rebuffs, my perseverance and my team's unwavering support made this triumph possible. I had proven to myself that I was breakproof.

I had reached the top of K2, and the mountain sang back to me.

BE BREAKPROOF: HOW TO RECOGNIZE WHEN IT ISN'T YOUR MOUNTAIN

1. **Understand the Landscape and Risks.** Each challenge or goal has its unique landscape and potential risks. It's essential to thoroughly research and understand these variables before embarking on your journey. This means understanding your physical, emotional, and logistical challenges and creating a solid plan to navigate them. Taking the time to learn about what you're up against can equip you with the knowledge to make informed decisions and reduce potential risks.

2. **Choose People Over Peaks.** In pursuit of a goal, it's essential to prioritize the safety and well-being of the people involved over the goal itself. Whether it's a business project or a mountain expedition, the safety and well-being of your team should always come first. This might involve pausing to make sure everyone is okay before making decisions that could put people at risk. In the long run, people will remember how you treated them much more than whether you achieved a particular goal.

3. **Know Your Team.** Understanding your team's strengths, weaknesses, and limits is crucial when undertaking challenging endeavors. This includes understanding everyone's skills, areas of expertise, and limitations. Doing so enables you to delegate tasks effectively, ensure that your team is functioning well, and provide the right support to your team members when needed. Trust in your team can significantly improve your chances of success.

4. **Value Life and Safety Over Success.** There will be times when the risk of pursuing a goal may outweigh its potential benefit. During these times, it's critical to prioritize your safety and the safety of those around you. Recognizing when to step back and potentially abandon the goal is a sign of maturity and wisdom, not weakness. Remember that no achievement is worth endangering lives.

5. **Give Back to Local Communities.** Wherever your journey
    takes you, make it a point to give back to the local community.
    This might mean hiring local workers, purchasing local
    goods, or supporting local initiatives. Not only does this
    help the local economy, but it also allows you to make
    meaningful connections and learn from the people who know
    the area best. This can lead to a more profound and more
    enriching experience.

6. **Understand and Respect Cultural Differences.**
    Understanding and respecting cultural differences is a
    cornerstone of successful teamwork, especially when the task
    at hand involves working closely with people from different
    backgrounds. Open dialogue about cultural expectations
    and norms can enhance team cohesion and mutual respect,
    fostering a productive working environment.

7. **Listen to Your Gut.** Sometimes, despite all the preparation
    and planning, something doesn't feel right. This gut feeling can
    be an invaluable tool for decision making. It's crucial to trust
    your instincts and consider turning back or changing course
    if something doesn't feel right. This might mean reevaluating
    a business decision or even aborting a dangerous climb if the
    conditions don't feel safe.

8. **Learn From Failures and Use Them as Stepping Stones.**
    Every failure provides valuable lessons to guide your decisions
    and actions. Instead of viewing failures as setbacks, see them as
    stepping stones leading to eventual success. The lessons learned
    from failure often provide the foundation for future triumphs.

9. **Cultivate Perseverance and Resilience.** Perseverance and
    resilience will carry you through the most challenging times.
    They enable you to pick yourself up after a failure, endure
    hardships, and remain committed to your goals despite
    adversity. Developing these traits requires a positive mindset
    and the determination to keep going, even when things
    seem impossible.

10. **Process Traumatic Experiences Before Involving Close Relationships.** A difficult or traumatic experience can be emotionally draining. Giving yourself time and space to process these experiences before involving your close relationships is essential. Use emotional-release mechanisms like journaling, artwork, or therapy to navigate your emotions. This approach allows you to come to terms with what happened, fosters healing, and helps you prepare to discuss your experiences when ready.

KNOWING WHEN TO STOP

You might find it odd that in a book named *BreakProof*, I'm touching on the idea of stopping. But here's the thing: stopping isn't the same as quitting. While quitting often connotes a finality—a sense of defeat—stopping can be a conscious decision—an acknowledgment that there's merit in pausing to reassess.

Imagine being on a long, demanding climb. Sometimes the wisest decision isn't to press ahead against raging storms but to find shelter and wait for clearer skies. This isn't giving up on the journey; it's ensuring you're in the best shape to continue. Persistent determination is commendable, but blind, unwavering persistence can be more harmful than beneficial, especially when conditions deteriorate.

Just like in a climb where blind persistence might cause injury or even death, in life, pushing forward without assessing our situation can backfire. Take the example of a workaholic so engrossed in their job that they overlook their own health or family ties: I know a brilliant but relentless engineer whose eighty-hour workweeks led to severe health issues and estrangement from his children. His "determination" cost him his health and connection with his family. That's not determination—it's recklessness. But there's another extreme: those so filled with doubt, they never even lace up their shoes to start. It's important to realize that there's a middle ground. You need to find a balance between these two extremes. It's about overcoming self-doubt, taking on challenges, and motivating you to reach your goals, but with a balanced perspective—giving yourself permission to stop when something is not working.

Sometimes the wisest decision isn't to press ahead against raging storms but to find shelter and wait for clearer skies.

Life will challenge us. Sometimes our setbacks are self-made, and sometimes they're out of our control. Maybe after pouring our hearts into a business, it doesn't gain traction. Or perhaps health challenges demand a shift in our careers. But in these scenarios, we shouldn't immediately see them as failures. They're merely signals that we might need to take a detour. This isn't about admitting defeat; it's about adaptability and resilience. Being breakproof isn't just about relentless forward motion; it's about knowing when to pause, recalibrate, and choose the best route—understanding that sometimes our journey to our summits is longer than we had hoped, and it might take us a few attempts to reach our destination in one piece.

People Are Always Ends, Never Means

You've heard me use the phrase "people over peaks" numerous times in this book. Now let's apply that to your own goals. Pause for a moment and ask yourself: "How many relationships am I willing to strain on my journey to achieve my goal?" Is the trade-off worth it? Is it worth scaling the summit if you're standing alone at the top, devoid of companionship and shared triumph?

It sounds like a ruthless question, and that's because it is. Sometimes we justify our behaviors, such as stepping on colleagues to get a promotion or overlooking others' feelings to get ahead, under the guise of improving our chances of success. Let me be clear: It is never worth it. Sacrificing trust and companionship for transient success leaves a void no achievement can fill. Your success doesn't have to come at someone else's expense. If it does, you should seriously rethink your strategy.

Competition is inherent to many goals, but how we compete matters. Imagine your goal isn't to start a business but to win a business award. I'm not suggesting you deliberately slow your pace to avoid obstructing a competitor's dreams, allowing them

How many relationships am I willing to strain on my journey to achieve my goal?

to move ahead and possibly win that award. I'm saying that striving to win an award shouldn't harm anyone else. In a competition, by definition, when one entity wins, another does not; this is the nature of awards. Most businesspeople aim to improve their operations, and awards are a common benchmark of such improvement. It's important to strive for excellence and pursue your goals vigorously. If everyone stepped aside for others, no one would ever win, which is a misunderstanding of the "people over peaks" philosophy. The issue arises when your pursuit involves undercutting or sabotaging another business to impede their progress. In that case, you are prioritizing your goals at the expense of others, which crosses an ethical line. You don't knock a fellow climber off a rope to reach the peak first.

When you chase your dreams while embodying the "people over peaks" philosophy—by considering the impact of your actions on others and choosing collaboration over ruthless competition—you contribute to a more ethical and harmonious environment for yourself and everyone around you. And if your path forward requires compromising the well-being of others, that's a clear signal to reevaluate your strategy and potentially choose a different, more considerate course of action.

At the core of the "people over peaks" philosophy is the fundamental principle that people are ends in themselves, not mere stepping stones to help us reach our objectives. When we treat people as mere instruments to achieve our goals—whether it's winning an award, securing a promotion, or building a business—we're devaluing their inherent worth. This perspective is ethically troubling and likely to foster a toxic culture that undermines our integrity and the sustainability of our successes.

By committing to a philosophy where people are valued as ends in themselves, we choose a path of respect, empathy, and collaboration— like a mountaineer who recognizes the value of every team member, understanding that the climb is safer and more rewarding when undertaken together. We affirm that our relationships—with colleagues, competitors, and community—are not disposable commodities to be traded for temporary victories but are vital aspects of a meaningful and fulfilling life. In this way, success becomes not a solitary peak reached at the expense of others but a shared journey that enriches our lives and the lives of those around us.

Knowing When to Turn Around

If it's acceptable to turn around when your safety is at risk, how can you determine when it is too great a risk to proceed? After all, whenever I set foot on a mountain, I exposed myself to various risks, including unpredictable weather, physical exhaustion, or potential avalanches. I didn't turn around every time that happened. Why did I decide to turn around on Broad Peak? And why *didn't* I turn around on other mountains that were arguably more difficult?

Knowing when to turn around comes from experience. Because I was more acquainted with weather tracking tech on my GPS device and I'd been in similar situations before, I knew trying to summit Broad Peak late in the day meant I'd likely get caught in a storm. Rick and I were the only ones who spoke up to turn around, and as a result, we were among the few climbers who avoided the incident on the mountain, when a climber fell into a crevasse and took the rope with him. I couldn't have imparted that knowledge to the other climbers except to voice my concern, and in the end, that wasn't enough to deter them.

And gaining experience from poor choices isn't always the best way to learn. It's unwise to face danger head-on just to recognize its perils for future reference. That would be terrible advice! "Go looking for trouble so you know how to identify it" is not the mantra you should live by.

A note of caution: Rick's tragic loss on K2 was a stark reminder that even the most experienced climbers are not immune to the unpredictable and unforgiving nature of the mountains. It reinforced my conviction that every decision to proceed or turn back must be made with the utmost care and respect for the risks involved. To honor Rick's legacy and contribution, I encourage others to adopt his cautious yet pioneering approach, respecting the mountain while also daring to explore new paths—literally on the slopes and metaphorically in life.

When deciding whether to turn around, one of the most valuable lessons I've learned is the importance of seeking guidance from those who have walked the path before you. Their wisdom and experience can be a lifesaving resource. I knew what weather patterns to look for and how to use my equipment correctly to avoid potential dangers and disasters because of the people who had taught me previously. Yes, some of it came from my previous experiences, but I never had to put myself in danger's way, because I had people around me when I started this journey who educated me on the dangers ahead.

Ask questions. This principle applies beyond mountaineering; consider, for instance, when you're opening up a small business. In the process of filing paperwork and securing loans for your small business, it's as crucial to ask others (and yourself), "What warning signs should I keep on my radar?"—such as a lender's unfavorable terms or a market that's oversaturated—as it is to ask, "What do I need to succeed?" By shifting your thinking to prioritize your safety—such as avoiding unsustainable debt or questionable partnerships—over mere hopes of rapid success, you'll be able to spot red flags earlier and decide whether to continue your ascent. This approach keeps you on a steady course, allowing you to recognize when to change tactics before catastrophe strikes.

However, don't use safety as an excuse for stagnation when things get tough. Avoiding risks entirely can mean missing out on deeply fulfilling experiences. For example, not attempting any of the Seven Second Summits would have meant risking living a life that wasn't fulfilling. We often acknowledge that our actions introduce risks, but our *inaction* is equally dangerous—don't get trapped, never leaving the house and never learning what you're capable of.

When deciding whether to turn around, one of the most valuable lessons I've learned is the importance of seeking guidance from those who have walked the path before you.

So how do we determine a balance? Trust your instincts and experience, lean on others for guidance and support, and be true to yourself: Will your decision allow you to expand and grow your capabilities? If your answer is yes, then you're becoming breakproof.

Start Your Grump Dump

Or a Downer Diary. Or a Slog Blog. Or a List of Lamentations.

Whatever you want to call it, don't bottle up the negativity.

Stuff goes wrong. Crap hits the fan. You won't dodge every curveball thrown your way. Not every hand you're dealt will be a winner. Ultimately, they all point to one truth: life's difficulties are inevitable. But they don't have to consume you.

When things go wrong, one of the best ways to deal with it is to get it out in the open. Staying frustrated doesn't help anyone, and it doesn't easily go away on its own. Anger and disappointment are like mold: they grow fastest in the dark. The Grump Dump—my journaling method—was how I handled frustration, disappointment, and difficulty. It was my way of putting it all out under the sun. It let me pull all my negativity out in the open so I could then burn it all away. This process isn't just metaphorical—it's a literal and psychological cleanse.

Whether this comes in the form of an actual diary, which can provide a tangible release; a list in your notes app, offering a quick and accessible outlet; or just venting to someone, which allows for empathy and support—it's important to get your feelings out of your head and into the world. This can give you a new perspective, helping you to understand and process your emotions more fully.

And then, let them go.

Get the feelings out, then let them turn to ash. Literally, if you want to. I burn each page of my Grump Dump as it gets filled, always ensuring I do so in a safe and controlled environment. If this isn't for you, consider other symbolic actions, like tearing the pages up or deleting the file, to signify letting those feelings go. This act of destruction is not about forgetting—it's about releasing. It's satisfying to watch what was irking me and gnawing at the back of my brain get turned into nothing. All the bad parts disappear. It reminds me that no matter how rough the present situation may be, this too shall pass—and my Grump Dump is a tool that helps me navigate those challenging times with resilience and grace. So start your own Grump Dump and take the first step toward turning your challenges into fuel for personal growth.

Come Back Stronger

So you've had to stop. You turned around and had to call it off for the time being. You didn't make it to the race, your business didn't get its footing, or your violin recital came and went without you.

That's tough. Now get back up.

We know it's easier said than done—setbacks are painful and can be deeply discouraging. Feeling down's normal, but allowing yourself to stay down won't help you progress.

Being breakproof—meaning being resilient in the face of the obstacles that arise on our journey to achieve a goal—is about getting back up. Some hardships knock you down, but you can always get back on your feet. Yes, you've had to stop, and that might hurt, but it doesn't have to stick. Let it slide off. Pick yourself up and get back in the ring. But make sure before you get in the ring that you've reflected on what went wrong, that you've learned and grown from your experiences, and that you're better than before.

It doesn't do you or anyone else any good to take another blind swing after quitting. If you've followed this book thus far, you should know not to give up lightly. You put in your best effort, and despite what you gave, you still came up short. You've turned to your Grump Dump and come out the other side with a brighter outlook. Now, you must do better and be better. This means analyzing your previous attempt by listing what went well and what didn't; identifying your weak points, perhaps by seeking feedback from a trusted colleague or mentor; and crafting a new strategy, which might involve setting new, achievable milestones and seeking additional training or resources.

Just as I spent a year between my K2 attempts climbing other mountains and researching how to tackle my nemesis better, a business owner might reevaluate their strategy, attend relevant workshops, or seek mentorship before launching a new venture. I didn't stop pursuing my goal and trained just as hard (if not harder), so when I faced it again, I knew I would be prepared for anything that K2 had to throw at me. I knew the path wouldn't be without incidents, but I prepared better to handle them. I improved my physical abilities by climbing other mountains. I gained more experience with peaks of a similar height and build. I researched more from those who had successfully summited K2 and assembled a team I knew was equipped to face the challenges that would most likely arise. I didn't get back up with the same strategy. I'd trained and adapted to know how to roll with whatever punches K2 threw my way.

When chasing your goals, keep in mind that you'll often get a second go at a failed attempt. Then the only question you must answer is "How will I do better?" Your first small business didn't launch and ended up folding. Due to a lack of interest or a poor marketing strategy, you couldn't turn a profit in the time frame you set for yourself, and things came crumbling down around you. But what will you do differently for your next small business? How will you redeem yourself? Do you need to find a different staff with a better marketing strategy for your target demographic? Do you need a more solid business plan to start? Should you consider taking a course in business management or finding a mentor in the industry? What funding goals could you reach to help get a solid start? Was your company culture askew, and could a change in philosophy help you grow faster and stronger? Who was the most helpful this first time around, and how could they assist you in this next attempt? Moreover, are there partnerships or collaborations that could boost your venture, and are there new markets or niches you hadn't considered before?

Make the necessary changes so you emerge stronger for your next attempt. And you will make another attempt. With resilience, determination, and a spirit of learning—and an openness to constructive criticism and feedback—you're becoming more breakproof with every step you take. Remember, every setback is a setup for a comeback, and your next move could be your best move yet.

// REFLECTION QUESTIONS

1. Have you reached a point in the journey toward your goal when you may need to face the painful truth that you need to take a step back, climb down from the metaphorical mountain, and take a different route? What evidence might help you decide that this is the case? Are there signs that your current strategy needs to be fixed, such as consistent negative feedback, declining performance metrics, or increasing stress levels? Consider the insights a mentor or trusted colleague might offer, such as alternate strategies or approaches you hadn't considered. How can their experiences and objectivity help you evaluate your situation more clearly?

_____

_____

_____

_____

_____

_____

_____

_____

_____

_____

2. Any big goal will come with its share of frustrations, setbacks, disappointments, and even regrets. What's your Grump Dump outlet to express any negative emotions and exorcize them from your psyche? Is it journaling, talking to a friend or therapist, exercising, or something else? How will having a Grump Dump process and tool help you build the positive resilience necessary to stay on course and finish the climb? How does regularly releasing your frustrations help you maintain mental clarity, reduce stress levels, and prevent burnout, enabling you to approach your goal with renewed energy and perspective?

    _____

    _____

    _____

    _____

    _____

3. Have you stalled on the journey toward your goal? What might you do to find the perseverance to try again? What steps can you take to reassess your approach, such as seeking advice, adjusting your timeline, or setting smaller, more achievable milestones? Can setting aside dedicated time for self-reflection and strategizing help you regain momentum? What might a dedicated self-reflection and strategizing session look like for you? Could it involve reviewing your progress, brainstorming new strategies, setting revised goals, or seeking external feedback? How regularly should you schedule these sessions?

    _____

    _____

    _____

    _____

    _____

4.   All meaningful journeys on the way to becoming breakproof
     involve change. How can you turn the inevitable failures into a
     catalyst for positive change? Can you identify specific lessons
     you've learned from each failure, and how can you apply
     these lessons to future endeavors? What is one failure you've
     experienced on your journey, and how can you reinterpret
     that event as a valuable lesson or a redirection toward a more
     promising path? Can you develop a practice of identifying the
     silver linings in each setback?

     _____

     _____

     _____

5.   What is the right size for your team? How will you know when
     you have too many? Are decisions bogged down due to
     excessive input, or is collaboration suffering due to overcrowded
     communication channels? How would you tell if you have too
     few? Are essential tasks falling by the wayside, or is your team
     consistently overworked and stressed? Is flexibility or skillfulness
     more critical in this task, and how can that inform you as to the
     size of your team? Do you need a team that can adapt quickly
     to changing circumstances, or is specialized knowledge
     and expertise more critical? If flexibility is your priority, what
     qualities or experiences should you look for when hiring team
     members, such as a varied skillset or a history of successfully
     adapting to new challenges? If skillfulness is the priority, should
     you seek individuals with deep expertise in a specific area,
     proven track records, or advanced training and certifications?
     How might you tailor your interview questions or candidate
     assessments accordingly?

     _____

     _____

     _____

     _____

CHAPTER 7

UNDERSTAND THAT THE GOAL IS NOT THE GOAL

OJOS DEL SALADO

Ojos del Salado stands as a silent guardian on the border between Chile and Argentina. As the only volcano of the Seven Second Summits, it towers at an impressive 6,893 meters (22,615 feet). Interestingly, it was the first on my list of Second Summits, not because of a strategic plan, but due to the serendipity of timing: the open climbing season aligned with my start. As the world grappled with the COVID-19 pandemic, Chile presented itself as an accessible gateway amid global closures, its borders more welcoming than many other destinations on my list.

Climbing Ojos del Salado is no walk in the park. The volcanic nature means a deceptive incline that constantly challenges climbers. Picture this: Every step you take, the volcanic soil beneath your feet gives way, ensuring a half slide back for every full step forward. It's like trying to race uphill on a sandy dune or fighting your way through a shifting gravel pit. That's the reality of Ojos del Salado.

This uphill battle, this eternal push and pull, reminds me of those never-ending projects we face at work or the personal challenges that keep pushing us back just when we feel we're making progress. It's a testament to the human spirit's tenacity. Just as it's essential to be breakproof on that mountain, it's crucial in life.

So let me take you on this journey, retracing my steps up Ojos del Salado. Let's navigate this together and find out where perseverance can take us.

We end where I began.

Raising My Sight

Believe it or not, when I decided to get into mountain climbing, I wasn't chasing any record. I didn't even know the title "First Woman to Complete the Seven Second Summits" was up for grabs. My sights were set on Ama Dablam, a Nepal peak near Everest. Well, not exactly neighboring—about nine miles apart—but both majestic Himalayan fixtures. The path to Mt. Everest takes you past Ama Dablam. Looking back, I realize how sometimes we aim for the achievable, thinking the colossal "Everests" of our lives are beyond our grasp.

The nudge that shifted my focus from Ama Dablam to the Seven Second Summits came from an unexpected source: my son. Life has a funny way of delivering inspiration, often when we least expect it and from unexpected quarters. One morning, while I was assisting him with his math homework, he wrestled with a tricky concept. I knew the struggle all too well from my schooldays. Ready to motivate him, I went into my "we do hard things" spiel, a mantra he was all too familiar with. As I waxed eloquently about aiming high and pushing limits, I could see his interest waning.

Then he blindsided me with a question: "If we're supposed to tackle hard things, why are you climbing a mountain named 'I'm a Dumb Blonde' instead of a real challenge like Mt. Everest?"

I had to chuckle at his mispronunciation. "First, it's Ama Dablam, not 'I'm a Dumb Blonde.' Second, get back to your sums," I retorted, trying to redirect the conversation. But his candid remark lingered in my mind. While I viewed any Himalayan climb as a significant accomplishment, it didn't register on his "awe" meter. Ama Dablam was an unknown entity to him. Would he be proud of a feat he didn't even recognize?

That casual chat sparked two resolutions. First, Mt. Everest was going on my list. Maybe not as the immediate challenge, but it was in the lineup. I contacted a seasoned climbing coach who felt he could prep me for Everest by the next climbing season. He kicked off my preparation on the spot, recommending a foundational climbing book.

My second vow was to explore the uncharted—to seek challenges I was oblivious to simply because I hadn't probed deeply enough. Interestingly, the coach's recommended book had an introduction about a woman who earned a Guinness World Record skiing across the Alps. When I mentioned this to my coach, he introduced me to another tantalizing possibility: the yet unclaimed (by a woman) Seven Second Summits.

You've probably figured out the sequel. A bit of digging, some pep talks, and I was gearing up to be the pioneering woman to tackle the Seven Second Summits. My game plan crystallized with my coach's guidance, a flurry of insights, and intense prep. And so, my odyssey commenced with Ojos del Salado, even though—fun fact—I had never slept in a tent before.

No Landmarks, Plenty of Wind

Ojos del Salado might not have been my primary choice for the inaugural peak of my journey (try saying that fast), but when the window of opportunity opened, I leaped through it. I had triumphantly scaled Ama Dablam, with Everest still beckoning, but its climbing season was a few months away. Still riding the adrenaline wave from Ama Dablam, I was itching for another ascent. Any of the Seven Second Summits would do. But the COVID-19 pandemic had slammed shut the doors of international travel, seemingly freezing my Seven Second Summits dream.

Then a ray of hope: Chile. Temporarily, with certain conditions, Chile opened its doors to travelers from the United States and beyond. Suddenly, Ojos del Salado was back on the map. Though it hadn't been my initial pick, the unpredictable nature of global travel made it my immediate priority. Would Chile's doors remain open? When would other countries follow suit? If I were to make headway on my goal, the moment was now. After a whirlwind of preparation, I found myself airborne, bound for South America.

Having already tasted the thrill atop Ama Dablam, I figured I had a grip on the essence of mountaineering. I couldn't have been more wrong. Utah might be my home with its own mountain splendor, but the Andes were an entirely different beast. The panorama was breathtaking. And since Chile had just reopened, locals perceived me not just as a tourist but as a beacon of hope, an indicator of better days ahead, a return to normalcy. This became a recurring theme on my travels. For instance, in Nepal, having landed mere days post their travel-ban lift, I was greeted and blessed by several lamas.

The journey to Ojos del Salado's base was uneventful. Yet, arriving there, I was greeted by an unusual sight—not the expected cluster of tents but two solitary shipping containers. Word to the wise: If your accommodation looks suspiciously like the back of a tractor trailer, brace yourself. The reason for this unconventional shelter? Tents stood no chance against Ojos del Salado's fierce winds. Though familiar with gusty conditions from my Midwest upbringing and skiing in Utah, nothing could've prepped me for the force I encountered there.

Ojos del Salado stands out, not just because it's a towering entity in the Andes but due to its isolation. Situated on

These small, persistent steps often lead to the grandest triumphs.

the Chile-Argentina frontier within the Atacama Desert, it rises, an unanticipated bump amid an otherwise even desert terrain: it looks like a zit. Born out of continuous volcanic activity, its ascent is a gradual yet unyielding incline. It boasts the title of the world's highest volcano, Chile's pinnacle, and South America's runner-up.

However, its desert location subjects it to dramatic temperature shifts and relentless winds.

Beyond the physical challenge, the monotony and desolation of the landscape took a toll on my mental stamina. The never-changing incline, paired with the vast stretches of sameness, became a mental labyrinth, forcing me to grapple with isolation, doubt, and the repetitiveness of the surroundings. Yet, it was amid this trial that my inner fortitude shone brightest. It was like tackling a long-term work project where the drudgery outstrips the actual challenge.

Did I mention the treacherous volcanic soil that constantly slipped beneath my feet? Each advance was countered by a slight retreat, almost like functioning at half throttle—one step forward, half a step back. The ascent might have been grueling, but mirroring life, these small, persistent steps often lead to the grandest triumphs.

Very Slow, Annoyingly Steady

The trek to Camp 1, the lone checkpoint between base camp and my towering goal, was more than a test of physical endurance—it was a mental gauntlet where the mountain often seemed secondary to my internal skirmishes, my doubts and fears. But it was also painfully repetitive. The drab colors amid scattered rocks painted a scene that left me underwhelmed. Much like the obstacles we face day to day, this ascent tested my grit and determination. I wasn't looking forward to Day 2 when we summited.

Trudging toward the summit, with guides at my side and nature's fury around, there were extended moments where I felt my mind turn traitor. Our early-morning push resembled a funeral march rather than a triumphant climb. Doubts loomed. Why was I subjecting myself to this relentless ascent? In contrast, Ama Dablam had been exhilarating. I'd been torn between admiring the stunning landscape of cascading peaks and the adrenaline of navigating one of the world's most challenging terrains.

Ojos del Salado felt like another world. If this was the benchmark for the Second Summits, what awaited me on the others? Was I in for a succession of slow, arduous climbs? I'd envisioned a thrilling journey, not this grinding test of will. Was it any wonder that so few had completed the Seven Second Summits? The stark barrenness of Ojos del Salado was worlds apart from Ama Dablam, making me question the path I'd embarked upon.

Yet, whenever thoughts of retreat crept in, I'd gaze upon the vast desert, realizing the rarity of my vantage point. I thought, "Wow! I may never get to see this desert from this angle again. I'm among a handful of people who have ever seen this desert like this." I belonged to an exclusive club that had witnessed this spectacle. This fleeting moment of wonder, brief as it was, realigned my focus. The panorama became a canvas, every memorable moment of the climb sketching its story—until I created a collage of determination and resilience.

The sky was a vivid shade of blue. The wind, though fierce, carried air so crisp it rejuvenated. My companions, a mix of guides and friends, became my lifeline, propelling me onward when my resolve waned. Against the backdrop of a global pandemic, here I was, living a dream in a foreign land. I was privileged to be on this unique journey and vowed not to mar it with trivial grievances. I was on an unparalleled adventure and committed to savoring every facet.

With each passing hour, the mental prison where I'd trapped myself transformed into a sanctuary. Gradually, each step forward replaced my grievances with gratitude as I steadfastly pressed on toward the horizon.

The End of the Beginning

I didn't always want to be a mountain climber. Passion, often a slow burn, evolves and morphs as we journey through life. Unlike those narratives that begin with "She's wanted to be a surgeon since age five," or "He was swaying to rhythms even before he took his first step," my path was less predetermined. I've always been someone who identified a goal and pursued it with unwavering tenacity.

However, the inception of a dream matters much less than its pursuit. And there I stood, having painstakingly scaled Ojos del Salado, with a panoramic view of the Chilean desert unfolding before me. Amid the biting winds and chilling cold, I stood victorious atop a mountain. This first daunting summit marked the commencement of an exhilarating journey. It represented not just a single conquest but an emblem of my determination, resolve, and bravery for the many climbs to come. I couldn't turn back now, and nothing in me wanted to. Beyond this peak lay more mountains, beckoning with fresh challenges. My motivation went beyond the titles and recognition; it was a testament to my children, showcasing my resilience and fortitude.

My journey was just beginning, but I could confidently say I was on my way.

BE BREAKPROOF: HOW TO UNDERSTAND THAT THE GOAL IS NOT THE GOAL

1. **Seek Opportunities in Obstacles.** Opportunities can often be found in unexpected places, and challenges can become stepping stones. Given the travel restrictions during the COVID-19 pandemic, Chile became the first accessible destination for my climbing journey. Despite its challenging terrain, I embraced it as an opportunity to start my journey of the Seven Second Summits. The goal is not merely reaching a destination, it's about finding the opportunities that come with the journey. Challenges and obstacles can be opportunities for growth if we're open to learning from them.

2. **Push Through Difficulties.** It's not just about achieving your goal but also about what you become by overcoming the challenges along the way. The challenging terrain threatened to slow my progress. Despite the difficulties, I didn't give up. Perseverance is essential to achieving goals, and challenges can be overcome with determination. The process of overcoming difficulties develops resilience and perseverance, which are valuable traits that transcend the specific goal.

3. **Seek Higher Goals.** Your initial goal can evolve. While my initial goal was to climb regional peaks, a conversation with my son inspired me to set my sights on the world's highest mountains. Always strive for more, and do not underestimate your potential; more extraordinary achievements may be within your reach. As we grow and gain new insights, it's important to reevaluate our goals and strive for greater achievements. The real reward is the process of continuous growth and self-improvement.

4. **Find Inspiration in Unexpected Places.** My goal to climb higher was directly inspired by a conversation with my son, proving that motivation often comes from the people closest to us. Motivation can come from unlikely sources; be open to inspiration from those around you. The true journey lies in

discovering these sources of inspiration and allowing them to guide your path.

5. **Make Resolutions and Stick to Them.** Sticking to a resolution is not only about achieving a specific outcome. It's about the discipline, commitment, and personal growth that come from maintaining resolve in the face of challenges. Motivated by my son's challenge, I resolved to climb Mt. Everest, ready to confront its unpredictable adversities. The power of determination can make even the most daunting resolutions achievable.

6. **Prepare for Mental and Physical Struggles.** The harsh conditions of Ojos del Salado challenged me both physically and mentally. Mental toughness is essential in overcoming life's hurdles; be prepared for both physical and mental struggles. The ability to prepare for and overcome these struggles is a transformative experience, which is more valuable than the achievement of the goal itself.

7. **Appreciate Unique Experiences.** The journey toward your goal will bring unique experiences that shape your perspective and understanding. My journey provided a distinct perspective of the desert landscape, which I sincerely appreciated. Exceptional experiences can offer valuable insights; embrace them for personal growth. They are an integral part of the journey, and appreciating them makes the process more rewarding than the goal.

8. **Combat Self-Doubt With Gratitude.** When self-doubt and fear threatened, I anchored myself by recalling the breathtaking sunrise I witnessed on Ojos del Salado. Positive thinking and gratitude can be powerful tools in overcoming self-doubt; focus on the positives in your journey. In striving toward a goal, self-doubt is a common obstacle. However, overcoming self-doubt through positivity and gratitude is a powerful personal transformation that extends beyond accomplishing the goal.

9. **Remember Why You Started.** When facing obstacles, I reminded myself why I embarked on the journey. In challenging times, grounding yourself in your original motivations can be

a beacon; hold on to the reasons you began. Recalling and reaffirming your "why" is a valuable part of your journey, often more important than reaching the end goal.

10. **Embrace Change and Adaptation.** Being open to new experiences and adaptable to changes in interests and goals can lead to exciting new paths; embrace change and adapt as needed. Life is unpredictable. While I hadn't always envisioned myself as a mountain climber, when the passion ignited, I embraced it wholeheartedly. Goals can change as we evolve, and that's perfectly fine. Embracing change and adapting to new goals is a part of the journey that signifies growth, making it more significant than clinging to an initial goal.

AFTER YOU SUCCEED

In reading this chapter, you might wonder, "Jenn, why is the final chapter about the first mountain you climbed? Doesn't that seem backward to you?" In a way, you have a point, and structuring it this way is not conventional. When we contemplate significant aspirations, we often envision them linearly—from inception to fruition. We lay out our dreams, marking the start and projecting a point when we'll realize them.

While such a linear approach offers clarity and specificity, it can sometimes box us in. After achieving a goal, it's crucial to ponder on the next steps. What lies beyond that pinnacle of success? After becoming the vision of yourself you've longed for, what follows? What's the next chapter after your triumph?

Hence, I end with the beginning—to illustrate that every culmination is merely a prelude to the next adventure.

Go for Tenfold

Initially, Ama Dablam represented the pinnacle of my mountain-climbing journey. Yet, with a gentle nudge from my son, I recalibrated my perspective. Perhaps I would have felt the same elation either way, but there's also the chance I might have later realized the grander vistas I overlooked. Regardless of the "what ifs," the experience enriched me.

As you approach the conclusion of this book, you've probably started considering your own goals. Maybe, since diving into these pages, you've put some plans in motion, eager to get into the driver's seat. But pause for a moment and reflect. How can you amplify this ambition? What zenith would you aim for if you weren't shackled by self-doubt or perceived inadequacies? Identify your "above and beyond." Now, shoot for that.

After achieving a goal, it's crucial to ponder on the next steps. What lies beyond that pinnacle of success?

To elevate my ambitions, I often contemplate what achieving ten times my current goal would entail. Essentially, what's my objective magnified tenfold? How challenging would that journey be? While some naturally harbor lofty dreams without such contemplation, others, like me, occasionally need to nudge ourselves to broaden our scope. Throughout this book, the concept of being breakproof consistently underscores the importance of continuous growth: *expanding and growing*.

Recall the prior chapter where I emphasized the benefits of specificity in goal setting. Well, refining your objectives not only attracts more assistance but might also introduce heightened challenges.

Imagine you're aiming to launch a local coffee shop. You've disclosed this ambition to a loved one, and they respond with news of an innovative, sustainable café model they've heard of. Opening a local coffee shop is commendable, and I'd never downplay that vision. But consider the broader possibilities. Why just one outlet? Why not a chain of eco-friendly coffee shops? Perhaps even pioneer a subscription model for gourmet-coffee delivery. Alternatively, consider merging your café with a co-working space, capitalizing on the rise of remote work. Whatever your endeavor, aim high and give it your all.

Start Small, Expect Boring

The grind. It's an inevitable part of the journey. Countless hours of routine tasks, preparation, or groundwork are looming between you and success. Let's face it: before you even hit the starting block, there's much groundwork awaiting you.

Expect boring. Expect pain. The initial steps are often the toughest, but powering through those challenges propels you toward your goal. If you're embarking on a business venture, many tasks must be tackled before "make your first sale" becomes a reality. And, sometimes, the process can feel repetitive and mind-numbing.

Consider this: In today's digital age, it's almost mandatory for businesses, whether sprawling corporations or startups, to have a social media footprint. If your food cart doesn't display its Instagram handle on its signboard, how will patrons share their experience or recommend your place? How will they stay updated on your specials or events? Establishing this digital presence is exhaustive. Regular updates, photo editing, video content, engaging captions, networking, interactive stories—it's relentless. It's a grind. But it's a necessary grind.

During my ascent of Ojos del Salado, I unearthed a fundamental tactic: Seek out the enjoyable parts of the grind. It might sound a tad clichéd, akin to "Chin up, buddy! Always see the silver lining!" And yes, it's somewhat in that vein. But it's effective. To be truly resilient—or breakproof—you need the grit to endure the long, arduous slog through the day-to-day grind.

But cut yourself some slack! You're chasing a vision! Sure, uploading your hundredth video on TikTok for the month might feel overdone, but reminisce about those positive responses from earlier uploads. Recall the satisfaction of perfectly editing that one clip. Milk the joy out of that for all its worth. Savor those victories, no matter how small, and let them fuel your perseverance. I promise, every small effort draws you nearer to your goal, and concentrating on the positives will help you get there more joyfully.

Have a Bad Memory

And here's the flip side of that coin. Things won't always go your way. Maybe you uploaded a negative video, encountered a harsh critique, or faced an onslaught of unfavorable feedback. Not a great feeling. Embrace that brief moment of disappointment. Then swiftly move on. This echoes a piece of wisdom an old pal imparted to me: Bruise hard, heal fast.

Reflecting on my expedition to Ojos del Salado, it struck me how much I'd inadvertently omitted from my recollection. The lingering memories were predominantly uplifting.

Picture this: When you're at a family gathering or walking in the park, when do you instinctively reach for your camera—in moments of distress, or moments of delight? Arguably, both can prompt a snapshot. Yet, most of us seize the moment to capture joy. Perhaps during your stroll, you spotted an owl nesting in a tree. Not groundbreaking, but a pleasing sight. Snap. The first blossoms of spring catch your eye. Snap. You bump into a long-lost friend and reminisce about old times. Selfie. Snap.

How often do you document those minor annoyances? Do you chronicle the dog that snarled at you, the tree stump you stubbed your toe on, or the unexpected downpour that drenched you?

Treat your memory like the gallery on your smartphone. Sure, there are times when the negative is so profound that it merits acknowledgment. That's valid. However, don't clutter your mental archive with trivial nuisances. Reserve that space for the myriad of delightful moments life offers.

The Beginning of the End

One day, you'll make it.

And then you'll reflect on that pivotal moment when you first shared your dream with someone, realizing how much time has passed and how far you've come. A surge of pride and relief will envelop you, as invigorating as that gulp of water after a challenging trek.

As we mature, our objectives shift, mirroring our life's various phases.

But when that initial euphoria of accomplishment fades, you might ponder, "Where do I go from here?"

If you're unlucky, this uncertainty following a goal can become an impediment, hindering you from progressing further. Without a new aspiration, there's a danger of undermining your accomplishments, clinging to a familiar ambition. Because without that goal, what defines you?

I've seen this in action more than once. When I ascended Mt. Everest, a feat many earmark for their lifetime, I observed a curious trend. Experienced climbers, for seemingly insignificant reasons, would opt to descend prematurely. The realization hit me: Their apprehension revolved around the looming question of "What's next?" After accomplishing such a monumental task, what remained for them?

I've never been solely focused on mountaineering. I've navigated numerous ambitions before and after. The driving force behind my professional and personal endeavors has evolved over time, a testament to my personal growth. Your purpose today might differ from the one you had as a child, a teenager, or a fresh graduate. As we mature, our objectives shift, mirroring our life's various phases. Embrace the diversity of experiences you'll encounter and ensure no single accomplishment overshadows the rest.

Each success sets the stage for a new adventure, and every journey springs from a preceding triumph. As you wrap up this book and crystallize your ambition, allocate a moment to contemplate what follows your goal's fruition. You've charted your path: the tasks, the strategies, the mentors, the resources. You've designed your routine with periodic introspections. And you've marked a deadline for your goal.

Now, plan for the day after. Or the week later. What could be next? Your subsequent goal might be something other than your recent success. Perhaps post mastering the violin, you're inclined to cultivate a garden. Maybe after completing a marathon, painting becomes your next muse. After your startup takes off, you could contemplate diversifying and expanding into a new market.

Alternatively, you could delve deeper into your passion, honing your expertise. Be it perfecting the violin, clinching a marathon victory, or scaling your enterprise, a realm of opportunities awaits. Whatever beckons you next, start laying the foundation today. There's always another dream shimmering in the distance. After every end, always find the courage to begin anew.

// REFLECTION QUESTIONS

1. You may be reading this book without a goal in mind or underway. And that's okay. What can you do to discover what you don't know about an area of interest, a long-held dream or desire, or a challenge that intrigues you? Brainstorm resources you could turn to and people you could engage with. Then see if that discovery process unearths something that feels like a meaningful and challenging course.

    _____

    _____

    _____

    _____

    _____

    _____

2. Do you need help in a section of your metaphorical climb that is boring, dull, bland, or otherwise demotivating? Think back to the elements of your journey that were the opposite: exciting, entertaining, rousing, or inspiring. Make a list of those moments. Expand on them to draft a mental mosaic by describing each with as much detail as you can remember. Place this difficult section within the larger context and look for how the highlights can inform and uplift you during the duller portions of your journey.

    _____

    _____

    _____

    _____

    _____

    _____

    _____

3. Once you've achieved your goal, what will come afterward? Write
    down what the day after you've reached your goal will look like.
    Then do the same for a week after, a month after, and a year after.
    What new, inspiring goal might you work toward at each interval?

    _____

    _____

    _____

    _____

    _____

    _____

4. What are the "snapshots" of poor memories or experiences
    you're holding onto that are getting in the way of your success?
    Take a moment to write them down, then crumple the paper up
    and throw it away, bury it, burn it, or otherwise destroy it. You get
    the idea. Do whatever it takes to "delete" those images from your
    camera reel and create a symbolic act representing the finality
    of your decision to move on from those harrowing memories.

    _____

    _____

    _____

    _____

    _____

    _____

    _____

    _____

5. Return to the previous reflection exercises in this book and complete those you skipped. Reread them all, paying attention to insights and learnings. Now make them actionable. Transfer those reflection questions that prompt you to action and schedule them in whatever system works best for you. Make specific commitments around what you are going to do and, if necessary, who you are going to reach out to and remain accountable to. This all contributes to your triumph in being breakproof. See you at the summit!

_____

_____

_____

_____

_____

_____

_____

_____

CONCLUSION

After my initial unsuccessful attempt at K2, the subsequent week in LA felt like a roller coaster. The remnants of the Grump Dump, blackened and charred, stood as a somber reminder of how life can throw curveballs when least expected. Every time I closed my eyes, vivid memories from the mountain replayed, haunting every quiet moment. All I wanted was the comforting embrace of my children, to lose myself in their innocence and joy. But with every memory of the mountain came a torrent of emotions, making me hesitate. Would I see my doubts and fears mirrored in their eyes? Would they sense my internal struggle and question it? Before I could face them, I needed to find my grounding, to remind myself of who I was beyond the mountain and its challenges.

Finally, I returned home where my children's unwavering joy awaited me, their infectious stories and laughter healing the void left by my recent trials. With every hug and bedtime story, I was reminded of our deep bond—a bond that had been immediate and unbreakable from the moment they came into this world. They have been the lights of my life, teaching me kindness, patience, and the true meaning of love. Their laughter and their lessons have anchored me more than any peak or expedition ever could. While the thrill of the climb, the allure of the unknown beckoned, the magnetic pull of motherhood was unparalleled.

It's only human to want answers, especially when those answers can't bridge the gap of longing. Why would I risk it all for a mountain? for an expedition? I've always believed that to live truly, one must embrace challenges, seek growth, and push boundaries. It's not about tempting fate but rather stepping into the fullness of life's potential. It's about not waiting for the "right moment" but seizing the day and living it to the fullest. And while the choices I've made might seem perplexing, the truth remains that I was driven by the urge to feel alive in every sense of the word, always with the intention of returning—of sharing tales of bravery and perseverance with my children. I wanted them to see firsthand the lessons learned from pushing themselves and embracing life's vastness.

Facing setbacks, whether on K2 or in life, we're all met with choices. One path is to retract, never face that challenge again, and let one's spirit be quashed by adversity. Another is to rise stronger, learn from past mistakes, and march forward with newfound wisdom and resilience. In sharing my journey with my children, I want them to recognize the strength that lies within them. I want them to understand that while life is unpredictable, it's also beautiful in its unpredictability.

I've always believed that my children are destined for greatness. And whatever they choose to do, wherever they decide to go, I hope my journey serves as a testament to the importance of living fully, passionately, and without reservations. Because life, with all its uncertainties, is too short to be lived in the shadows.

And so, as this book draws to a close, I am left with one final thought: To be breakproof is not just about never giving up but about living with intention, purpose, and boundless love. Always.

Mango Publishing, established in 2014, publishes an eclectic list of books by diverse authors—both new and established voices— on topics ranging from business, personal growth, women's empowerment, LGBTQ studies, health, and spirituality to history, popular culture, time management, decluttering, lifestyle, mental wellness, aging, and sustainable living. We were named 2019 *and* 2020's #1 fastest growing independent publisher by *Publishers Weekly*. Our success is driven by our main goal, which is to publish high-quality books that will entertain readers as well as make a positive difference in their lives.

Our readers are our most important resource; we value your input, suggestions, and ideas. We'd love to hear from you—after all, we are publishing books for you!

Please stay in touch with us and follow us at:
Facebook: Mango Publishing
Twitter: @MangoPublishing
Instagram: @MangoPublishing
LinkedIn: Mango Publishing
Pinterest: Mango Publishing

Newsletter: mangopublishinggroup.com/newsletter

Join us on Mango's journey to reinvent publishing, one book at a time.

BREAKPROOF

JENN DRUMMOND

Seven Children. Seven Continents. Seven Summits

Jenn Drummond achieved business success as the founder and CEO of a thriving financial services company in Park City, Utah. It was there that her family's passion for everything outdoors, from hiking and biking to skiing and mountain climbing, really took root.

However, on a snowy evening in 2018, Jenn's life was knocked off its tracks. She was in a horrific car accident that brought her inches from death. All the authorities and experts agreed that she shouldn't have survived, yet somehow she did. In the aftermath of that brush with death, it became crystal clear to Jenn that while she can't control when she dies, she—and the rest of us—can choose how we live.

Jenn's confrontation with death imbued her with vigor, enthusiasm, and commitment for full engagement in life. Now, more than ever, she is focused on becoming an inspiration, a guide, and a cheerleader not just for her own children, but for all of us.

As a world-record holder, an author, and a thought leader, she now spends her time inspiring others to live a life of significance.

JOIN A 40-DAY CHALLENGE!

RECOVERY & RECHARGE

High-level professionals often fall prey to a constant charge without an appreciative pause. In this challenge, we'll take a modest moment to look back on where we've been and what we've accomplished. We'll banish the daily blinders that have us "going through the motions," and bring our body, mind, and soul back to center so we can replenish and be ready for the next big opportunity.

PARENTING

Each time I left home for a summit attempt, there was a sense of excitement for the adventure ahead but also an overwhelming doubt. I felt like a terrible mom, even though my kids were enthusiastically cheering me on from home base. In this challenge, we'll dive into our lives as parents, and I'll share sound strategies I've learned for balancing your life and needs both outside and inside the home.

LEADERSHIP

Before deciding to go for a world record, I had already built a successful business. I knew there was more to life, and my original quest has now become my mantra: "from a life of success to a life of significance." In this challenge, I'll share with you the powerful principles that helped me bolster my business, master the mountains, and determine my destiny.

EVEREST

Join us as we embark on this virtual collective challenge, climbing 29,029 feet over the course of 40 days (from the comfort of your own home!). With each step of the challenge, you'll face new obstacles and overcome new challenges, just like a real climb. Along the way, you'll gain insights into what it takes to make it to the top. You'll learn how to get your vertical feet in at home and receive cross-training workouts to build strength, endurance, resilience, and mobility.

SPEAKING EVENTS

What does climbing have to do with corporate life?

You don't need a brush with death to become BreakProof. Long before I was conquering mountains, I was blazing a path of my own as I built my own business.

With over 28 years of real-world experience in financial services, I know what it takes to set goals, achieve the seemingly impossible, and build and lead teams as part of a wildly successful business venture.

And more than that, I've distilled my decades of experience and lessons down into an instantly applicable mindset—a behavioral and process-driven toolkit to help you and your team become BreakProof.

Because failure, setbacks, and challenges are all part of the journey to the top.

For speaking opportunities, please contact the Gray + Miller Agency

GRAY +
MILLER
AGENCY

949.245.7940 | inquiry@graymilleragency.com